DATE DUE		
	JAN 2 '00		

AUTHORS TEENS LOVE

Joan Lowery Nixon

Masterful Mystery Writer

Mary Dodson Wade

Enslow Publishers, Inc.

40 Industrial Road   PO Box 38
Box 398   Aldershot
Berkeley Heights, NJ 07922   Hants GU12 6BP
USA   UK

http://www.enslow.com

*In memory of the lovely lady who is the subject of this book
and especially for Nick
and the rest of her beautiful family*

Library of Congress Cataloging-in-Publication Data

Wade, Mary Dodson.
    Joan Lowery Nixon : mystery writer / Mary Dodson Wade.
       v. cm. — (Authors teens love)
    Includes bibliographical references and index.
    Contents: Ideas out of the ordinary—Reading at age three—Published
author—Family matters—Make them shiver—The heart of history—Fun
and facts—Consider the children—The gift of reading—In their own words.
    ISBN 0-7660-2194-7
    1. Nixon, Joan Lowery—Juvenile literature. 2. Authors, American—
20th century—Biography—Juvenile literature. 3. Detective and mystery
stories—Authorship—Juvenile literature. 4. Young adult fiction—
Authorship—Juvenile literature. [1. Nixon, Joan Lowery. 2. Authors,
American. 3. Women—Biography.] I. Title. II. Series.
    PS3564.I946Z97 2004
    813'.54—dc22

                  2003027484

Printed in the United States of America

10 9 8 7 6 5 4 3 2 1

Photos and Illustrations: All photos courtesy of Joan Lowery Nixon.

Cover Illustration: Courtesy of Joan Lowery Nixon (foreground); Carl
Feryok (background).

Contents

Foreword

Writing this book was one of the easiest projects I've ever done. Joan Lowery Nixon graciously shared stories about herself, her books and her writing career.

The editor at Enslow was enthusiastic when I suggested a book about Joan for their "Authors Teens Love" series. For me, it was an opportunity to write about someone I knew personally and admired professionally.

I first met Joan in 1978 when I took her class on writing for children. As a librarian, I knew books, but she knew how to write them. I was in awe. I still have the incredibly organized set of notes from that class. It was my start in writing for children.

Through the years I followed her career as she turned out an enormous number of books by sheer dent of discipline. It didn't hurt that her mind seemed to see a story in every situation.

She had a wonderful sense of humor and often chuckled as she related things that happened to her. But she was serious about her profession and very supportive of beginning writers. It was typical of Joan to volunteer to mentor a deserving author each year.

I knew of Joan's devotion to her family, but only in working on this book did I learn the many things she had done to change the lives of young people—the "Kids Love A Mystery Week" to encourage kids to read and create stories, the writing badge for the Girl Scouts of America. She was especially fond of two books showing teen mothers how to love and discipline small children. Joan wrote the books and raised money for printing because it was important to her that the books be given free of charge.

She had read the manuscript for this book before pancreatic cancer took her life. Her death has left me with a tremendous sense of loss, both personally and professionally. I could find no better example to follow.

Mary Dodson Wade

CHAPTER 1

Ideas Out of the Ordinary

A haunted plantation—the perfect place for a mystery writer! Joan Lowery Nixon's daughter-in-law, Allyson Nixon, read an article about a haunted Louisiana plantation. On weekends the owner of "The Myrtles" opened his home for ghost tours. Allyson Nixon and her husband, Joe, invited Joan and Hershell Nixon to share the spooky experience with them.

After a candlelight dinner, guests toured the grounds. The host explained various ghosts that haunted "The Myrtles." The ghost in the bedroom where the elder Nixons slept was a house servant who had murdered family members. The weeping figure was often seen rocking a baby near the window.[1]

Alas, mystery writer Nixon went to sleep and missed the ghost. But her mind was working just the same. "What if a ghost was so terrifying that no one would set foot inside the house?" From those thoughts came *The Haunting*. The main character finds the courage to enter the house in spite of the horrifying ghost. *The Haunting* is classic Nixon fare—"a hint of romance, some really scary scenes, and a plucky heroine who successfully routs both outer and inner demons."[2]

Nixon was creating stories and poems long before she was old enough to read or write. Her family were all avid readers. Young Joan sensed the value of words at a very early age. She would come to her mother and say, "I have a poem. Write it down."[3]

It helped that her imagination worked overtime. Even when she was very young, she would think *What if. . . .* The habit has become almost subconscious. *What if*s pop up even when she doesn't intend them to happen. In late 2002, she was working on a book called *Laugh Until You Cry*. It was not supposed to be a mystery, but the final version ended up that way. "Most of my stories turn into mysteries," she said with a laugh.[4]

Joan Lowery Nixon grew up in Hollywood, California. At the age of ten she had a poem published in a children's magazine. Her first payment for writing came when she was seventeen. It was her high school teacher who encouraged her to choose journalism as a college major.

While in college she met Hershell Nixon. They were married after he finished a hitch in the Navy. He was a geologist, and they lived in several states because of his work. Even after four children arrived, Joan managed to write magazine articles.

A move to Corpus Christi, Texas, led to her career as a children's book author. Nixon attended a writing conference there in 1961. Three years later, her first book, *The Mystery of Hurricane Castle*, was published.[5]

She was serious about her writing career. She bought bookends and placed a note between them that said, "Watch this space grow!" Mary Blount Christian, a close friend, made the decision to write as well. Instead of bookends, though, Christian bought a large trash can to hold her rejection slips. She too has published over 100 books, but she laughs about her trash can. In those early years, it was much more useful than bookends. "I doubt her [Nixon's] bookends are strong enough to hold all those books now, but then she has plenty of awards to hold them, too."[6]

In the 1980s when Nixon's career was hitting full stride, she longed for more writing time. At lunch one day, a cousin asked what she wanted for Christmas. Without hesitating Nixon replied, "An extra hour in each day, an extra day in each week, and an extra week in each month." The cousin worked for a large computer company. A computer seemed the perfect answer. But Nixon gasped at the price—the computer cost as much as a car. Hershell Nixon encouraged his wife to buy it.[7]

> "I doubt her [Nixon's] bookends are strong enough to hold all those books now."
> —Mary Blount Christian

When the computer came, she was overwhelmed by all the things she needed to know. She signed up for a class to learn to use the new machine. Two weeks later

Joan, like most authors, relied on a computer for story writing and research.

she was happily adding or deleting text on the computer. Best of all, she could move text without retyping it.

Nixon now has two computers in her office. The older one is a dedicated word processor. It produces text only. She creates most of her stories on it. The other computer has lots of "bells and whistles." She writes some stories on it and uses it for e-mail and Internet research.[8]

Most writers develop a routine that makes the writing process easier for them. Nixon gets up at 6 A.M. She reads the *Houston Chronicle* at the breakfast table. After a 15–20 minute session on the treadmill, she heads to her office in sweat suit and sandals at 8:30 A.M.[9]

Writer/Rewriter

"I rewrite as much as I write. I am constantly rewriting and editing and polishing what I've written, so I was positive that the computer had been invented just for writers."[10]

First, she checks e-mail. Then she rereads the previous day's output and begins writing new passages. Some people like to listen to music as they create, but Nixon works in silence—no music or radio. She sits surrounded by stacks of resources in a room her daughter Eileen Nixon McGowan describes as "frighteningly overloaded with documents and books."[11]

Having a routine gets rid of many distractions, but it does not guarantee that writing will be easy. "Some days everything just flows so fast I can't believe how many pages I have written. Other days it's like pulling words out of my head with a pair of pliers."[12]

She works until noon, then fixes lunch for herself and her husband. Afterwards, she settles down with a book—often a mystery—and reads herself to sleep. After a short nap, she might go back to the computer. Sometimes she runs errands, and on other days granddaughter Katie McGowan comes to the house after school.[13]

Many authors keep a journal to help them recapture information and emotions. Nixon does not. Instead, she tucks clippings from magazines and newspapers into a file folder. She cuts out articles that grab her attention and places them in the filing cabinet. When she needs an idea, she takes the folder to her bed and spreads out the contents. She looks over the clippings and begins to think *what if. . . .*[14]

By 2003 Nixon had written 138 books. Over half of them are mysteries. She writes two to five books a year. It takes about three months to do the actual writing after the story has been planned in her mind.[15]

She researches everything, even fiction. If she is writing a mystery, she usually sets it in Texas. Police procedures vary from place to place. In Houston, where the Nixons moved in 1974, police are used to her questions.[16]

Research takes her to interesting places. She has been locked inside the women's jail in Corpus Christi; bent over to crawl through a cavern; walked a Civil War battlefield in Missouri; found out from the crew how Mississippi River paddlewheelers work; and, of course, spent the night at a haunted plantation. Visiting the sites of her stories often reveals things that book research cannot do. *High Trail to Danger* is set in the mining town of Leadville, Colorado. She discovered that walking in Leadville's thin air made her wheeze. Her character does the same.[17]

In order to make her books more realistic, Joan often traveled to gather information. Here, she is in Haiti while doing research for a book called, *Playing for Keeps*.

When she chooses a character's name, she considers the character's personality and the time period. First names come from a book called *What to Name Your Baby*. Sometimes Nixon checks street maps for suitable last names.[18]

Students often ask which is her favorite book. Her answer is always the same—the one that she is working on right then. She is living with those characters at that moment. "I'm a storyteller. With each book I tell a story through the eyes and voice of my main character, so each book is different."[19]

She places great emphasis on developing her main character. She gets inside the main character's head in order to write the story. This ability to portray teenagers is one of Nixon's strong points. "Her characters come alive by reflecting the flaws and foibles of the teens who read the books."[20]

Nixon grabs readers at the opening of the story, then hangs on to them by giving them someone they can relate to. One fan commented, "I got so involved in the story I thought I was Stacy."[21]

In her mystery stories, the main character has two problems to solve. One is a personal problem. The other is the mystery to be solved. Nixon thinks of her books as novels with mysteries buried in them.[22]

Some writers begin a story without knowing the ending. They develop the story as they write. Nixon

Emotions

Generation to generation emotions don't change. Loneliness, fear, joy, sorrow, embarrassment.... External situations may differ greatly, but the emotions they cause are always the same.[23]

never starts a story until she knows how it ends. She does not want to write 200 pages and then be unable to finish the story logically.[24]

The middle of the story is where she has room to expand and change. "My stories are like a ball of clay. All the things I want for the story are in the ball of clay, but they haven't been formed yet."[25]

Nixon's method worked well for her. The space between the bookends grew. Awards began coming about ten years into her career. The first came when the Texas Institute of Letters chose *The Alligator Under the Bed* as 1975's best juvenile book.[26]

Among the medals and plaques in the den of her

Houston, Texas, home are four statuettes. They are Edgars—whimsical ceramic likenesses of Edgar Allen Poe. Mystery Writers of America awards Edgars each year to the best mystery books. Nixon has won four of them in the juvenile/young adult category. Five other titles of hers have also been nominated for the Edgar Award.[27]

"Murder and chicken salad are a normal part of the Nixon household," says Eileen McGowan. She knows because she has worked with her mother creating mystery events to present for various organizations. One such event took place aboard a Cunard cruise liner. As part of the entertainment during the voyage, passengers could examine evidence left at a "crime scene" and solve a mystery.

McGowan and her mother met to plan for the event. Over lunch in an upscale restaurant, they earnestly discussed how to kill someone without leaving visible signs such as blood. They debated whether to use poison or to suffocate the victim.

In the middle of this the man at the next table jumped up and raced over to the waitress. McGowan watched his frantic whispered conversation. She leaned over and told her mother that the man thought they were planning a murder. "Of course, we are, sweetheart," replied her mother. "We want to make this as realistic as possible." When Nixon finally understood the situation, she announced in a loud voice, "Oh, plotting these murder mystery events can be so difficult!" The man never returned to finish his meal, and the waitress kept close watch on the "murderers."[28]

Nixon's books and awards are not limited to mysteries. Two of her historical novels in the Orphan Train Adventure series won Spur Awards. This award is given each year by Western Writers of America to honor outstanding juvenile fiction about the American West. Three other Nixon books have been Spur finalists.[29]

Honors are now coming for her entire collection of works. Her sense of humor shines through when she mentions receiving a lifetime award from Southwest Mystery and Suspense Writers several years ago. "I kind of wish they would have waited about 10 years for that one. My lifetime's not quite over yet."[30]

In fact, she keeps producing books and winning awards. In 2002 Nixon was honored with the Kerlan Award from the University of Minnesota. Eighty of her books are in the Kerlan Collection. This collection is a place where authors and illustrators deposit manuscripts and art related to the creation of a book. Researchers use these materials to follow a book from idea to finished product.[31]

A second 2002 award came from the Catholic Library Association. Nixon received the St. Katharine Drexel Award for outstanding contribution to the field of young adult literature.[32]

Nixon is happy that adults like her books, but she cherishes the awards that come from children. In many states children choose a favorite book each year. Children in twelve states have honored Nixon's books a total of nineteen times. She is a three-time winner in Virginia and Indiana.[33]

Perhaps one of her fans expressed it best. "Dear Mrs. Nixon, Your books are stolen out of our library more than any other author's. Does that make you feel good or what?"[34]

CHAPTER 2

Reading at Age Three

Growing up in Hollywood, California, would be a dream existence for most people. For Joan Lowery Nixon it was a reality. She was born in Los Angeles and grew up in the movie capital of the world. She saw nothing unusual about living in a neighborhood of movie stars and directors.

The Lowery family car had belonged to movie idol Adolph Menjou. The car was like a limousine. It had jump seats and a glass partition that rolled up between the front and back seats. Joan's father bought the car because it had room for the whole family to ride together.[1]

The family included Joan, her parents, her two sisters, and her mother's parents. Joan's father, Joseph Michael Lowery, was an accountant. Joan's mother, Margaret Meyer Lowery, had been a kindergarten

Growing up in Hollywood was fun for Joan. Acting and being imaginative were qualities admired not only in the town, but also in the Lowery household.

teacher. Joan, their first child, was born on February 3, 1927.[2]

Several years later, Joan's sisters Marilyn and then Patricia arrived. Their house on the corner of 73rd Street and Gramercy was a duplex. Joan's bedroom was on the side with her grandparents. Her sisters shared the second bedroom on her parents' side. The two parts of the house were connected by a room where the girls could play.[3]

Mrs. Lowery had been a Montessori kindergarten teacher. The playroom was filled with things that encouraged creativity. There was a piano. The girls had crayons and a large board on which they could draw and color. They molded clay, cut construction paper, drew pictures, and wrote stories. The cupboards were full of puzzles and games. Mr. Lowery built a large doll-house that was filled with furniture and dolls.[4]

All three girls eventually became writers. Middle sister Marilyn Lowery has written romance novels. Youngest sister Patricia Lowery Collins is an artist who also writes poetry and books for young people.[5]

Creativity

"A good imagination was so highly prized (in our family) that for a long while I thought it was a measure of intelligence."

—Pat Lowery Nixon.[6]

Mrs. Lowery wanted to be a model mother. She joined a woman's group called the Cornelia Club. The club had social activities, but one of its objectives was to help the women be better mothers. Joan was well cared for. A photograph of her at two years of age appeared in the *Los Angeles Evening Herald*. She had been named the "Healthiest Baby in Los Angeles." She won the title two years in a row.[7]

As the only grandchild for three years, Joan was the center of attention. Everyone read books to her. One of her favorite memories is of her grandfather, Mathias Meyer. He was a retired postman who loved books of great literature. Regardless of what he was reading, he would stop and let Joan crawl into his lap.[8]

Joan could probably have read the book herself, but she preferred her grandfather's lap. Fox Movietone News filmed three-year-old Joan reading. These short films were shown in theaters before the main feature started.[9]

Mrs. Lowery bought a large scrapbook and filled it with pictures of Joan. In several photos, Joan looks very much like a dark-haired Shirley Temple. She was about the same age as the famous child movie star. Included in the scrapbook are stories and poems that Joan wrote.[10]

After her sisters came along, Joan became something of a neighborhood ringleader. She was in the thick of rowdy weed fights. The children pulled up long strands of oat grass and threw it at each other. Weed fights were especially good after a rain made the ground soft.[11]

Another favorite game was called "First Light." When Joan was growing up in Los Angeles, it was safe to play outside after dark. The game was timed to the street lights. The first person to see the street light turn on shouted, "First Light!" That person got to tag everyone else on the arm.[12]

Roller skating was a great pastime as well. Joan

swooped down their long driveway, up into the neighbor's drive, and kept going.[13]

As she got a little older, she put on shows with the dolls in their doll house. Neighborhood children waited eagerly for Joan's stories. When word got out that she

Fox Movietone News

Nixon got a wonderful surprise in 2002. The film department of the University of South Carolina was restoring Movietone films made from 1918 to 1935. These included out-takes, the part not shown in the final version. The film editor saw an out-take with the title, "Joan Lowery, Age 3." She thought that the child in the film might be children's writer Joan Lowery Nixon. The studio did not have the finished film of Joan reading, but they duplicated ten minutes of out-takes and sent Nixon a copy. She showed it to her grandchildren. They found it very funny to watch their Grandma as a little girl.[14]

was doing a show, a steady stream of children knocked on the Lowery door to find out when the show would be.

On the day of the big event, children filed into the playroom to sit in front of the three-sided doll house. Through Joan's storytelling magic, the small ceramic dolls changed into characters with exciting adventures. No two stories were alike. The dolls became different personalities with each show.[15]

Using the dolls as characters fit well with the puppet shows the family produced. Mr. Lowery built the puppet theater. Mrs. Lowery wrote scripts based on

Joan's mother encouraged her daughters to be creative. Their puppet shows were enjoyed among children throughout the city.

well-known stories such as Peter Rabbit and Punch and Judy. While the two older girls worked puppets behind the stage, youngest sister Pat often sat in the audience. She talked to the puppets as part of the act. The December 22, 1935, issue of *The Los Angeles Times* carried a feature about the shows that were presented at children's hospitals, orphanages, and schools.[16]

A puppet presentation to a group of Japanese children gave Joan direction for her future career as a writer. The very young children could not understand a word that was said. Still, they laughed at the puppets. Joan was fascinated. "I realized that day the power of 'story telling'. . . these little ones, unable to understand the dialogue, still responded. . . with as much enthusiasm as any audience we had ever met."[17]

In addition to the puppet shows, the Lowery girls took expression and dance classes. At recitals they performed dances and recited poems. Mrs. Lowery made their costumes. At one performance Joan sang the Raggedy Andy song "I've Got a Pain in my Sawdust."[18]

Among the stories Mrs. Lowery put in Joan's scrapbook is one Joan wrote at age nine. It is called "A Trip to Fairyland." Her family still teases her about it. Joan wrote the story after Mrs. Lowery asked her daughters what they wanted to be when they grew up. Marilyn answered that she wanted to be a plain mother. Joan piped up, "Oh, I'm going to be a lady who's raring to go."[19]

Her family knows that is just what she has done. Decades later she is still raring to go—writing and giving speeches.

CHAPTER 3

Published Author!

Some authors wait nearly a lifetime to see their name in print. For Joan Lowery Nixon it came much sooner. A page in a children's magazine called *Children's Activities* featured stories and poems written by youngsters. Joan was ten when she wrote a poem called "Springtime." It appeared in the April 1938 issue.[1]

Joan attended elementary school at Seventy-Fourth Street Elementary School only two blocks from her house. She was a good student, but math gave her a little trouble. Her father helped her think through the problems, but he never told her the answers.[2]

She was an eager participant in activities like paper drives. Grandfather Meyer had built a large wooden wagon for the girls. Joan and Marilyn pulled this through the neighborhood to collect newspapers.

Patricia, too young to help, became a human paperweight on top of the stack of papers.[3]

For two years Joan attended Horace Mann Junior High. An article in the May 24, 1940, issue of the

---

"Springtime"

Springtime is the time of the year

When birds begin to sing

And children play outdoors

Because they're glad it's spring.

The leaves start budding on the trees.

The grass begins to grow.

And everybody's happy

Because it's spring, you know!

—Joan Lowery, age ten[4]

---

school newspaper, *The Wise Mann*, described the Lowery family puppet shows. The reporter asked Joan whether she wanted to continue giving puppet shows. The answer was prophetic. "Joan doesn't plan on making puppeteering her life career. Her great ambition is to write children's books and later to become a kindergarten teacher." She would eventually follow both careers, but she did them in reverse.[5]

It was about this time that her beloved Grandfather

In this photo, taken when Joan and her family moved in with her grandmother, are (from left) Joan, Marilyn, Grandma Meyer, Patricia, and Mrs. Lowery.

Meyer died. Joan's father had an important job as auditor-comptroller for Los Angeles County. He handled money for the whole county. The family moved to a large house in a fancy section of East Hollywood called Laughlin Park. Joan shared a bedroom with her grandmother. From the window she could see the lights of Hollywood theaters.[6]

Many famous people lived in this section of the city. Lowery neighbors included movie director Cecil B. DeMille, comedian W. C. Fields, and prizefighting champion Jack Dempsey. Fields was not one of Joan's favorite neighbors. He often drank too much and said cross things to people who passed his house. De Mille lived across the street from Fields, and he made up for Field's grumpiness. He always tipped his hat to Joan when she walked up the hill from school. She thought it was such an elegant thing to do.[7]

Moving to the new house meant that Joan was a total stranger when she entered ninth grade at Le Conte Junior High. She felt so alone the first day. Then she met Mary Lou Weghorst, another new student. They quickly became like sisters and began a lasting friendship. Mary Lou's house was only a mile away. The two friends walked back and forth to visit. They adopted nicknames for each other. Mary Lou became Mufty. Joan was Johnny.[8]

The next year the two friends entered the huge Hollywood High School. Joan and Mary Lou did not have many classes together because Joan was on the academic (college) track. Mary Lou was on the secretarial track. But they were inseparable out of class. One time

Classes with Hollywood Actors

"Many of my schoolmates were in the movies. Someone would disappear and not be back for the rest of the year because they had parts in a film. They were taught on the set. But we had the best school plays because of all those out-of-work actors."[9]

they sneaked into W. C. Fields's estate and took photographs of themselves. In the summer they took the street car to the beach to swim. They went on long bicycle rides.[10]

It was not unusual to run into movie stars. One afternoon Joan and her friends were in an ice cream shop when Shirley Temple came in. Joan's crowd pretended they did not see her. They didn't want people to think that they stared at movie stars.[11]

Singer Frank Sinatra had all the teenage girls screaming. Joan went to a Frank Sinatra radio show. She thought the screaming was silly. She wondered whether the girls had been paid to act like that.[12]

When Joan and Mary Lou began dating boys, several couples went out together. They would go to places like the Mexican shops on Olvera Street, one of the original streets in Los Angeles. Sometimes they went to Chinatown.[13]

When she was a high school sophomore, nearby Los Angeles Junior College gave a Sadie Hawkins dance. At Sadie Hawkins dances, the girls invite the boys. Joan was excited about going with a boy named Marcus, but she did not know him very well. That night she wore a new white pinafore dress, trimmed in red, with tiny red apples on it. Mr. Lowery drove them to the dance, saying he would return when it was over at 11 P.M. Plans for a lively evening fell apart when Joan and Marcus walked in the door. The room was decorated with bales of hay. Marcus began to sneeze and sniffle so badly that he had to go outside. Joan, to be polite, went outside with him. She expected to spend a very long evening waiting for her father to return.

Marcus insisted that she go back inside, but that was not much fun either. She had no one to dance with. Then, suddenly, the tempo of the music picked up. The crowd formed one large circle. A guy rushing past grabbed her hand. "A girl as pretty as you shouldn't be left watching," he said. She never found out who he was, but she still remembers his kindness. The memory of her feelings at this age influence her writing today.[14]

World War II had started the year Joan entered high school. Families wanted to help servicemen who were far away from home. On Sundays Mr. and Mrs. Lowery invited young men to their house. "My mother's theory was that any boy away from home who went to church was probably a good boy, so she and my father would linger after Mass was over to invite to dinner any servicemen who had been attending Mass."[16]

Remembering How It Felt

"I also remember very distinctly how I felt at that age."[15]

When the young servicemen came, Joan called Mary Lou and a few other girlfriends. They played shuffleboard, ping pong, badminton, and tetherball outside. Inside there was pool and pinball. Sometimes they rolled up the living room rug, put on a stack of records, and danced. Often, the servicemen called to ask if they could come again the next weekend. This went on until they were shipped out.[17]

Meanwhile Joan never stopped writing. Her poems filled birthday and greeting cards for friends and relatives. Holidays and family celebrations were occasions for new poems.

High school friends, especially, called on her talents. The girls wanted to write to servicemen after they left for duty. Joan was in great demand. She would create a romantic poem every couple of weeks. All the girls would copy the poem. The same poem went to many different servicemen.[18]

Americans helped in the war effort by planting "victory gardens." People grew vegetables in their

Joan and her best friend, Mary Lou (left), were inseparable during their high school years.

yards and gardens. Mr. Lowery asked his daughter for help. "Can you write me a poem on victory gardens?" He used her poem in a talk.[19]

Joan's mother needed to prepare a program for the Cornelia Club. "I have to speak about adolescent girls," she said, "and there's no way in the world that I understand adolescent girls."

Joan reassured her mother. "Don't worry about it. I'll write your speech for you." Mrs. Lowery appeared before her friends and gave the speech that Joan had written.[20]

Tall, black-haired Joan joined the high school drill team. One Christmas, the weather turned very cold for the parade. Mrs. Lowery insisted that she wear a blanket under her costume. Joan was stuffed into her uniform. She was embarrassed because a boy she liked would be there to watch her. He surprised her later by telling her how nice she looked in the parade. What he did not know was that he had been watching the wrong girl! Another tall girl wore her dark hair the same way as Joan. They looked very much alike.[22]

"Mufty Is Sixteen"

Mary Lou's sixteenth birthday prompted a poem from Joan.

If I weren't angelic and also true blue

I'd be awfully jealous of you, Mary Lou!

Gee whiz! What have you got that I haven't got?

Well, technically speaking, really a lot.

You look good in sweaters, your chassis's a whiz,

And your `line´ is a masterpiece—certainly is.

You could be a stand-in for some lovely star,

Or else be the actress. That's better by far.

Your cooking is good, and you sew—with some aid.

Your boyfriends are many; you're a popular maid.

Yes, you always surpass me, but this is the worst.

You left me behind and became sixteen first!

—Joan Lowery (Nixon)[21]

Joan's father later made the same mistake while taking pictures of her graduation in the Hollywood Bowl. He was too far away to tell her from the other girl.[23]

While at Hollywood High School Joan had an English teacher who influenced her career more than anyone else. Bertha Standfast recognized Joan's talent for writing. She praised her student's work. "You have talent. You're going to be a writer."[24]

Miss Standfast strongly urged Joan to study journalism in college, but Mr. Lowery objected. The only journalists he knew were newspaper people who interviewed him. They made a bad impression because they drank a lot. Joan's father did not want his daughter associating with such people. Joan, however, did not want to be a newspaper reporter. She wanted to be a war correspondent. But the war ended before that could happen.[25]

She was a seventeen and a freshman in college when she first received money for her writing. She had seen a copy of *Ford Times*, a magazine sent to owners of Ford cars. Joan knew that she could write articles like those in the magazine. She pretended that she was a mother and wrote about ways to entertain children on trips. Soon she had her first check—$35. She thought, "This beats babysitting."[26]

CHAPTER 4

Family Matters

One week after graduating from high school, Joan enrolled at the University of Southern California (USC). She followed her teacher's suggestion and majored in journalism in spite of her father's objections. She believes that journalism played a big part in her success as an author. She was required to use a typewriter—no one had personal computers or laptops at that time. Journalism classes forced her to think and create at the keyboard. Even exams were taken on a typewriter.[1]

Journalism taught her to focus on a subject, to research and organize material. For each news story, she answered the basic questions *Who, What, When, Where,* and *How.* These same questions are useful in writing fiction.[2]

During college Joan wrote a fashion column for the school newspaper, *The Daily Trojan.* As part of her journalism training, she worked on the staff of a fan magazine called "Hollywood Entertainers." Because she was young, she was assigned to interview starlets. She did not drive, but boys from one of the fraternity houses across the street were more than glad to help. It gave them the opportunity to be near glamourous starlets. Most of the ones she interviewed never became famous. The exception was the dancer Cyd Charisse.[3]

While still in college, Joan became interested in writing radio scripts. Her mother suggested a night

Creativity

"(Journalism) teaches you to apply the seat of the pants to the chair and work even if inspiration doesn't strike. I had a teacher argue with me when I said that to students. She felt that creative writing only came with inspiration. Inspiration is only the beginning. The manuscript has to be written and that takes work."[4]

course being offered at Hollywood High School. Not wanting her daughter to travel alone on the streetcar at night, Mrs. Lowery enrolled in the class too. As things turned out, Joan was too busy with her college courses to continue. Mrs. Lowery, however, had found her niche. She began producing scripts for many of the top dramatic radio programs.[5]

Joan joined Phrateres, a service organization. Phrateres sponsored projects that raised money for things like the girls' sports program. One event was a fashion show, and Joan wrote the script for it.[6]

She also spent time at the Red Cross hut on campus. There were 10,000 sailors and marines in the V-12 program at USC. This program offered accelerated classes so that servicemen graduated in three years. At the Red Cross hut servicemen could get buttons sewed on their uniforms and hems fixed while they waited.[7]

During her freshman year Joan pledged Kappa Delta Sorority and is still active in the organization. She has served as president of the Kappa Delta Houston Day Alumnae Association.

In her senior year a sorority sister suggested that she could arrange a date for Joan with Hershell Nixon. Nick, as he was called, was in the Navy V-12 program. Friends thought they would make a good couple. Joan knew that Nick had been dating a sorority sister. She did not feel right about going out with him. Then she learned that Nick and the girl had broken up. Nick invited Joan to go with him to the Orchid Ball. At this special dance all the girls wore baby orchids. Two weeks later, Joan and Nick were engaged.[8]

Almost immediately Nick left for a ten month tour of duty in China. When he came home, he brought with him enough white satin for Joan's wedding dress. But he still had several more months of duty in Hawaii. During his absence, Joan had the material beaded and made into her wedding dress. Finally, Nick's naval duty was over. Joan Lowery and Hershell Nixon were married on August 6, 1949.[9]

Joan's degree in journalism did not help her find a job in that field. War correspondents returning after World War II had taken those positions. In contrast, the Los Angeles school system desperately needed teachers.

Joan's wedding dress was handmade from satin that Hershell had brought back with him from China.

Joan was hired as a kindergarten teacher. By day, she taught kindergarten at Ramona Elementary School. In the evening she took education classes at Los Angeles City College. By the time her husband earned a degree in geology at USC in 1952, their daughter Kathleen was two years old.[10]

Hershell Nixon went to work for an oil company. As a geologist, he explored remote areas for likely places to drill for oil. The Nixons moved to Billings, Montana. Because geologists worked in the field during the summer, the company encouraged employees to take along their families. One summer the Nixons lived in a room at a little motel in Bridger, Montana. There was no kitchen, so everyone ate in the cafe. The menu seemed to be only meat and potatoes. Joan requested a salad. The waitress appeared with potato salad.[11]

Because there was little to do, Joan and Kathy sometimes went with the men while they were surveying rock formations. The car had no air-conditioning. On one trip they were sitting in the back seat with the windows down. A swarm of grasshoppers flew in. While Kathy screamed, Joan frantically fought off the grasshoppers. The other geologist threatened to leave them at the motel if they were going to act like that.[12]

While they were staying in Circle, Montana, Kathy broke out in a rash. The Nixons learned that the water in the town had been contaminated. Twice a week they drove fifty miles to buy water to drink.[13]

In spite of this, Joan loved the beautiful Rocky Mountain scenery. Joan met the owner and the only resident of Maiden, Montana. She used Maiden as the setting for a fiction story in *Ghost Town*.[14]

The Nixons moved frequently after returning to California. Maureen, their second daughter, was born in Los Angeles in 1954. Two years later, son Joe was

Hershell and Joan Nixon lived in a number of places because of his job as a geologist. Their family eventually grew to include Kathleen, Maureen, Joe, and Eileen.

born in Ventura. In 1958, youngest daughter Eileen was born in San Mateo. Even with small children Joan Lowery Nixon managed to find time to write for magazines.[15]

Then in 1960, the Nixons moved to Corpus Christi, Texas. It was a struggle for her to leave California. But moving to this new home marked the beginning of her career as a children's book author.

Chapter 5

Make Them Shiver

Mysteries have played a large part in Joan Nixon's life since she was quite young. At six, unknown to her parents, she listened to "I Love a Mystery" radio programs. Later she carried around Nancy Drew books. In high school she read Raymond Chandler and Agatha Christie because there were no young adult mysteries. Her pleasure reading now includes books by Sue Grafton, Aaron Elkins, Nevada Barr, and Sharyn McCrumb.[1]

More than seventy-five of her books are mysteries, and the number continues to grow. The books are praised for "graceful writing, taut suspense, and rich characterizations." Both the quantity and quality of her books have earned her the title "Grande Dame of Young Adult Mysteries." The four Edgars peering out from the bookcases in her den mark her as the only author to have won the Mystery Writers of America top award four times in the juvenile/young adult categories.[2]

It all began when Nixon attended the 1961 Southwest Writers' Conference in Corpus Christi, Texas. Several of those who attended, including Nixon, were interested in writing for children. The ten aspiring authors agreed to meet every Wednesday for lunch. They brought manuscripts and listened as each was read. Those listening offered suggestions and encouragement.[3]

Nixon shared information about magazines that might buy what they wrote. She knew these markets because she was selling to them. Writing time had been scarce with four young children, but Mrs. Lowery offered to pay for a housekeeper one day a week. While the housekeeper watched the two preschool children, Nixon shut herself up in the back bedroom. Soon she was selling stories and articles to children's magazines and some adult religious magazines.[4]

One of her best markets was a Hollywood teen magazine. On one particular day, she received a check from the magazine. In the same mail was a letter from a magazine published by a boys' orphanage in Chicago. The editor explained that he had run out of money to pay authors. He asked if Nixon would allow them to print her story anyway. He promised that the boys would remember her in their prayers. Four-year-old Joe was very impressed. He announced to the neighbors, "Mama is very happy. Some man in Hollywood is sending her money, and all the orphans in Chicago are praying for her."[5]

When Nixon mentioned the idea of writing a book, Kathy and Maureen talked it over and gave her firm directions. "We've decided. If you're going to write for children, you have to write a book, and it has to be a mystery, and you have to put us in it."[6]

There was little to guide Nixon. The librarian found one book for her—Phyllis Whitney's *Writing for Children*. Whitney had won the very first juvenile Edgar award. Nixon studied Whitney's book to learn how to make her own book interesting.[7]

She loosely based *The Mystery of Hurricane Castle* on the family's experience of moving to the Texas Gulf Coast during a hurricane. In the story, the Nickson children—Kathy, Maureen, and younger brother Danny—are stranded in a house that is said to be haunted.

> **It all began when Nixon attended the 1961 Southwest Writers' Conference in Corpus Christi, Texas. Several of those who attended, including Nixon, were interested in writing for children.**

As the story developed, Nixon read it to the family each night after dinner. She always stopped with the cliffhanger at the end of a chapter. The children begged her to stay up and write the next chapter so that they could know what happened. Kathy suggested that she put in something funny. A reviewer called *Mystery of Hurricane Castle* a "very friendly, spooky story."[8]

Once the manuscript was finished, Nixon submitted it to twelve different publishers. Finally it was accepted by Criterion Press. Nixon laughs now at her novice mistake. The editor told her that she would have called to say she wanted to publish the book, but there was no telephone number on the manuscript.[9]

In the next seven years, Nixon sold five more mysteries to Criterion Press. Eileen starred in the second book, *The Mystery of the Grinning Idol*. The story is about smuggled Mexican artifacts. The Nickson girls appeared again in *The Mystery of the Hidden Cockatoo*. It featured a gold-encrusted pin that had been lost in the New Orleans French Quarter. Joe's turn came in *The Mystery of the Secret Stowaway*.[10]

Between 1979 and 1981 she published seven easy-to-read holiday mysteries for Albert Whitman. In 1975 Nixon and daughter Kathleen attended the first International Crime Writers Congress in London, England. The speaker suggested that Nixon try an older audience. That began her collection of Edgars.[11]

In 1980 she won her first Edgar for *The Kidnapping of Christina Lattimore*. The story was inspired by the kidnapping of Frank Sinatra's son. His kidnappers claimed that he planned the whole thing in order to get money. In Nixon's story, Christina is frustrated because people believe she arranged her own kidnapping in order to get money from her grandmother.[12]

Just one year later Nixon received a second Edgar for *The Séance*. It was inspired by Maureen's seventh grade sleep-over party. At the party, the girls held a séance. They decided to try to talk to Walt Disney's ghost because he did not seem so scary. Nixon's story, however, is very serious. The lights go out during a séance behind locked doors. When the lights come back on, one of the girls is missing. Later she is found dead. The main character believes that she is the person the murderer is seeking.[13]

After the awards ceremony was over, an elated

The Edgar Awards, presented each year by the Mystery Writers of America for the best mystery stories, is named for Edgar Allen Poe. Joan Nixon is pictured with three of her Edgars, above.

Nixon entered the elevator clutching her statuette. The woman standing next to her offered congratulations but added, "You've done so well with your books for children, why don't you try writing a *real* book." Nixon explained that it was harder to write children's books. Young people would not read books that failed to keep their interest.[14]

The Other Side of Dark earned Nixon her third Edgar in the juvenile category. The 1986 winner was based on an article Nixon read about a young man who lay in a coma for four years after an accident. His mother believed he would wake up. She massaged and exercised his muscles. Nixon began to think about teenagers and all the changes that happen during that period of a person's life. What if a thirteen-year-old girl was shot and her mother killed? What if the girl woke up four years later in the body of a seventeen-year-old? What if the murderer is stalking her?[15]

The Other Side of Dark was a huge success. Children in California, Colorado, Iowa, Oklahoma, Utah, and Virginia chose it as their favorite book. In 1995 the story was turned into an NBC Monday Night Movie called *Awake to Danger*.[16]

The movie version changed more than just the title of the story. Nixon's plots are tight with accurate details. When she received a copy of the script, there were holes in the mystery. She called the studio to point out some ways to fix illogical incidents, but the movie had already been filmed. She discovered that the script had gone through twenty re-writes. Only the first writer read her book. A second revision changed the first script. Each revision changed the previous script. Nobody went back to the book.[17]

The action of the main character at the end of the movie particularly bothered the author. As the girl faces grave danger, she calls, "Help! Help! Help!" Someone rushes in to save her. Nixon always lets her characters work out their own problems.

Nixon's fourth Edgar came in 1994. *The Name of the Game Was Murder* won the young adult category. In the story, the main character helps celebrities solve the murder of a book author and remove information about themselves from his book.

In addition to the books that received Edgars, five others were finalists for the award—*The Mysterious Red Tape Gang* (1975), *The Ghosts of Now* (1985), *The Weekend Was Murder!* (1993), *Shadowmaker* (1995), and *Spirit Seeker* (1996). In addition, Nixon served as a judge ten times. That took her book out of competition for the prize those years.[18]

In the meantime the Nixon children grew up and married. Kathleen Nixon Brush, Maureen Nixon Quinlan, Joe Nixon, and Eileen Nixon McGowan have given Joan and Hershell Nixon thirteen grandchildren. The grandchildren began to appear in Nixon's stories. In 1991 granddaughter Nicole (Nikki) Brush starred in the four light-hearted Nic-Nac mysteries about some young journalists. Melia Brush appeared in *If I Were a*

No "Help! Help! Help!" Heroines

"I write about strong girls. They may not be the brightest in their class, but they've got good common sense. And they may be scared to death, but they do something about it. And they are not going to go screaming, "Help, Help! Help!" They're going to think of what they're going to do to save themselves."[19]

Writer. Grandsons Brian and Sean Quinlan were the two young detectives in the twelve *Casebuster* stories that appeared 1995 to 1997. Nixon borrowed Andy Quinlan's name for *Search for Shadowman*.[20]

The Nixons often take family vacations that include the grandchildren. One year they went with the Quinlans to Disneyworld. The *Casebuster* series was going strong, and everyone wore T-shirts with "I'm a Casebuster" printed on them. People kept asking about the Casebusters. Sean, who was nine at the time, thought it took too long to explain about his Grandma writing the books. He told Brian just to tell them Sean was a star.[21]

Joan and Hershell Nixon were known as Grandma and Papa to their thirteen grandchildren, many of whom are shown here.

Nixon is serious about getting the facts correct in her stories. She took a cruise to prepare to write *Playing for Keeps*. The story involves a Cuban baseball player who stows away on a ship in order to escape. She discussed with the chief of security where someone might hide. She examined the holding cell. The officer explained that the holding cell was used mainly to let people sleep off the effects of drinking too much alcohol. Nixon discussed ways for her character to get on board. The chief of security's eyes got wide as she described her plan. He reluctantly admitted that it would work, but he did not want to advertise that fact. "We're not in the business of aiding stowaways."[22]

Much closer to home, she used the foyer of her Houston home as the setting for *Whispers from the Dead*. Tall panes of glass beside the front door allow visitors to see into the hall. *Whispers from the Dead* grew out of a real murder that happened in Nixon's neighborhood. A young woman delivering mail was dragged into a house and killed.

Nixon's idea file helped shape *Whispers from the Dead*. One clipping told about people who unknowingly bought houses in which murders had occurred. From the same file she used an article about experiments at the University of California at Los Angeles (UCLA) psychology department. The staff at UCLA interviewed people who had near-death experiences. For several months afterward, these individuals felt a warm, comforting presence with them.[23]

In Nixon's book, Sarah's family finds that they have moved into a house where a pizza delivery girl has been murdered. Sarah has survived a near-death experience and is contacted by a ghost who speaks only Spanish. That allows Sarah to solve not one, but two murders.

The murder that spawned *Whispers from the Dead* continues to bother Nixon. She is convinced that there were two murders. The young man's confession mentioned throwing the body in the bayou, but the mail carrier was found in a field miles away. Nixon believes the mail carrier saw the other murder and was killed to keep her silent. When Nixon mentioned inconsistencies to a homicide detective, he shrugged. It was not his case. Nixon suspects that the police really did not want to listen to a mystery writer.[24]

A Deadly Game of Magic was sparked by an incident involving Nixon's parents. The Lowerys were driving one evening when they had car trouble. They approached a house to make a phone call, and the man invited them inside. He and his wife were leaving for a party, but the Lowerys were welcome to stay until the tow truck arrived. Nixon was horrified that her parents would enter the house. Her mind began racing. *What if* the people they met were really burglars? *What if* there was a dead body in the back room? In *A Deadly Game of Magic* four high school students have car trouble as they return from a speech tournament. They are invited into the house by burglars who leave. Rising water traps them there. All the while an evil magician is playing deadly games with them.[25]

Students tell Nixon that her two scariest books are *A Deadly Game of Magic* and *The House on Hackman's Hill*. She got the idea for mummies in *The House on Hackman's Hill* from a visit to the Los Angeles museum.[26]

Whether lighthearted or deadly serious, Nixon's books are favorites with young people. Teachers use her books to snare reluctant readers. Parents love her books because she can create suspense without using gore, drugs, or sex scenes.[27]

Nixon has a unique way of thinking about mysteries. She believes that people read mysteries, not to be scared, but to be reassured. "You read the newspapers about all the crimes. . . . But a mystery is always solved. The bad guy is always arrested and sent to jail or bumped off. You're safe."[28]

Scared or safe, readers thrive on Nixon's mysteries that are "distinguished by stalwart female protagonists and a gradual, carefully built rise in tension."[29]

Chapter 6

The Heart of History

Anyone who thinks that Joan Lowery Nixon writes only mysteries has missed a large segment of her books. Readers of her historical fiction find stories that touch their hearts.

To Nixon, history is more than a collection of dates and events. Children have always been present at historical events. The appeal of Nixon's historical books comes from telling the story through the eyes of a child.[1]

The Orphan Train series grew out of a terrible problem in this country. There were no child services available in the 1850s. Immigrants in New York City slums worked long hours in factories. There was little money for food. Babies were abandoned. Homeless, neglected children roamed the streets. They begged or stole to have something to eat.

Charles Loring Brace founded the Children's Aid

Society to help these children. His program sent them to live on farms in the west. Adult chaperones rode trains with the children. At each stop, the children filed out onto the platform. Local families looked them over and decided whether to take a child home with them. The children who were not chosen returned to the train. At the next stop, they filed out on the platform again.[2]

> **"The main character is always the most important part of any novel—not the period, not the place, not the history."[3]**

A program of this type would not be allowed today. Nobody at that time understood how hard it would be for the children to grow up without knowing what happened to their family. The idea of placing children in other homes, however, was the start of foster care in this country. The orphan train program ended when state and local agencies took charge of neglected children. Child labor laws and compulsory education also brought an end to the practice.[4]

The Children's Aid Society tried to make sure the children would be treated well. Families who took them were to be moral people who promised to provide good care. The children were to be treated as part of the family. They would get enough to eat. While helping with farm chores, they would get exercise and fresh air.[5]

The first orphan train left New York City in 1853. By the time the last one ran in 1929, the Children's

Aid Society had placed more than 120,000 children in foster homes. The trains went to forty-five states as well as Canada and Mexico. During the early years Indiana received more children than any other state.[6]

The New York Foundling Home, a Catholic agency, sent out another 100,000 children. These children went to prearranged homes to insure that they were placed with Catholic families.[7]

In many cases, the situation was a happy one. Some of the children became very successful people. Two became state governors. In other cases, the child was simply someone to help with hard work. There was no love, and shortcomings brought severe punishment.[8]

After the orphan train program ended, it was quietly forgotten. Nixon was unaware of it until her agent's husband called in 1986. His company developed books for large publishers. He had just read an article about the orphan trains and thought the topic would make a great series of books. But who could write them? He and his wife both said at the same time, "Joan Nixon." After learning about orphan train children, she knew immediately that she had to write about them.[9]

Nixon began research in New York City at the Children's Aid Society. She devoured materials she found in the archives of the society. She read about different children and their circumstances. She learned about the backgrounds and traits of families who took the children. There were journals kept by the adults who traveled on the trains with the children. She found letters from both agents and children.

Among the reports from agents who went to check on the children, there were stories that tugged at her heart. Four-year-old Willie was a problem child who had been placed with a childless German couple. Agents usually returned in six months to check on the children. In Willie's case, the agent went back in three months. He expected the couple to shove the hard-to-manage child at him. Instead, they informed him that they had no intention of sending Willie back. The agent asked why they wanted to keep him. "It's simple," they said, "We love him."[10]

Working with these materials, Nixon put together a "bible" for the series. This overall outline explained who the characters were and what each book would cover. She planned four books in the Orphan Train series to tell the story of the Kelly children. Bantam won the bidding to publish the books.[12]

> "I have got to write these books. This is just very, very moving."[11]

About this time the Orphan Train Heritage Society of America was organized in Springdale, Arkansas. Mary Ellen Johnson had put out a call for family stories to help her write a history of the area. One man responded about a relative who had come on an orphan train to Springdale. Johnson began to pursue orphan train riders and their stories. The society she founded publishes their stories. Members come seeking lost relatives.[13]

Nixon joined the Orphan Train Heritage Society and was invited to speak at the first annual meeting in 1987. She listened to stories about brothers and sisters being separated. One man at the meeting held up a picture of a little boy. "I haven't seen him since I was eight years old. Has anyone seen my brother?"[14]

The first book in the series, *A Family Apart*, had just been published. Nixon was signing copies when an elderly orphan train rider was introduced to her. Before autographing the book, Nixon asked if that was the name she wanted in the book. The woman hesitated and said, "No." She had just found out that her mother had named her Jesse. She wanted the book inscribed with the name her mother had given her.[15]

Nixon's Orphan Train stories begin just prior to the Civil War. The six Kelly children–Frances Mary, Michael Patrick (Mike), Megan, Danny, Peg, and Petey–are put on the orphan train. Mike had been caught stealing food for the family. Thirteen-year-old Frances Mary, the oldest, is hurt by her mother's decision. Nixon, as a mother of four, had trouble herself with the idea of giving away children. She tried to imagine how the mother felt. She has Frances Mary ask her mother how she could do this. Mrs. Kelly answers, "Oh, Frances Mary, don't you realize? It's because I love you so much that I'm able to send you away!"[16]

Nixon read this part of the book at the society meeting. Afterwards an eighty-year-old man came up to her. He said, "I always wondered why my mother gave me away. Now I know." Several years later, a young Vietnamese girl who had been adopted by American parents wrote Nixon to say the same thing.[17]

In *A Family Apart*, Frances Mary disguises herself as a boy in order to stay with Petey, the youngest child. *In the Face of Danger* places Megan in the home of a kind, young Kansas couple. When tragedy comes, Megan believes that she is the cause. Western Writers of America honored these two books with Spur Awards in 1988 and 1989.[18]

Caught in the Act, the third book, finds Mike in an abusive home in North Dakota. In the fourth book, *A Place to Belong*, Danny and Peg live with a kind Swedish family. When Mrs. Swenson dies, Danny schemes to have Mr. Swenson marry their mother.

The popularity of the books prompted the editor to

ask for three more. These are set during the Civil War. Nixon uses the turmoil of the time to weave history into the stories. *A Dangerous Promise* tells how Mike escapes his abusive family, lies about his age, and joins the Union Army as a drummer boy. *Keeping Secrets* has Peg Kelly aiding a female Union spy at a time when women could cross enemy lines. Both these books were finalists for the Western Writers of America Spur Award the years they were published.[19]

Circle of Love is the last book in the Orphan Train Adventures series. Seventeen-year-old Frances Mary is now the chaperone for a group of children. This book introduces the characters for the Orphan Train Children series.[20]

This series for younger children takes place after the Civil War is over. *Lucy's Wish* is about a girl who wants a sister, but the sister is not the perfect one Lucy imagined. In *Will's Choice*, Will's father cannot take care of him. Will is torn between returning to his circus performing father or staying with the kindly doctor and his wife. Aggie in *Aggie's Home* is an abandoned child who lives at the Asylum for Homeless Waifs. She finds a home with an elderly couple. *David's Search* brings David face-to-face with the evil of racism shown by the Ku Klux Klan, a hate organization.

When Nixon was asked to speak at the Texas Book Festival several years ago, she invited two orphan train riders to appear with her. They were in their eighties and very exited to meet then-governor George W. Bush and Mrs. Bush. When it came time for their presentation, the room was packed. One of the women brought tears to many eyes when she held up a tiny coat. "This is the coat I wore when I was on the orphan train."[21]

During the question and answer period, the woman seemed amazed by the question asking whether she

Joan was invited to speak at many different conferences and meetings, not only because of her writing, but because of her commitment to important causes, like children's rights and good parenting.

had to work hard. The spunky lady replied, "Yes. . . but everybody worked hard. We lived on a farm!" She drew applause when she added, "If they made the kids today work as hard as we did, they wouldn't be in all this trouble."[22]

Nixon is proud that the books brought attention to orphan train riders. Iowa schools use her books to highlight that part of their state history. They held a statewide celebration honoring orphan train riders.[23]

After the success of the Orphan Train books, Nixon's editor approached her about writing three books featuring young immigrant women. Ellis Island, where immigrants arrived on the East Coast, was being restored at that time. The editor knew that three of Nixon's grandparents had come to this country from European countries.

The editor wanted the girls to be on the same boat so that they could meet each other. She asked that the first girl be Jewish and settle in the garment district in New York. She wanted the second girl to be Irish, like Nixon's grandparents. In *Land of Hope*, Nixon brings Rebekah's Jewish family to America to escape persecution. They work long hours in the garment factories and live in crowded tenement houses. Rosie, in *Land of Promise*, goes to Chicago as Nixon's grandparents did. She works to help bring over her mother and sisters. Nixon chose a Swedish girl as the third heroine. In *Land of Dreams* Kristin's family has come to farm free land in Minnesota, but independent-minded Kristin wants more freedom for herself as well.[24]

Nixon's reputation for writing historical fiction led the editor of publications at Colonial Williamsburg to contact her. The editor wanted a series of books about children who lived during colonial times.

Williamsburg, Virginia, was the capital of our

country while it was still part of England. The city had parliament buildings and taverns. Two hundred years later, it was a sleepy village with greasy service stations next to the priceless old buildings. Millionaire John D. Rockefeller poured money into restoration. All the modern things were cleared away. Experts researched documents to restore everything just as it was before the American Revolution. Records showed who lived there, what they owned, and how they lived. Today Williamsburg is a place of living history. Visitors meet people in costumes who have assumed the roles of those who lived in Colonial Williamsburg.

Before going to Williamsburg, Nixon poured over boxes of material that had been sent to her. Then she spent a week in Williamsburg absorbing the scene. The books are about children who really lived there. Historians told her everything about the family—their names, where they lived, whether they were rich or poor, who their friends might be. Every subject had a special historian. There was one for food, another for clothing.[25]

Getting Facts Correct

"Whatever entered into that book, they had that expert check it out. Everything in those books is totally, totally accurate. And that part I like."[26]

The Colonial Williamsburg editor planned four books with boys as main characters and only two with girls. Nixon asked that it be three and three. *Ann's Story: 1747, Caesar's Story: 1759, Nancy's Story:*

1765, Will's Story: 1771, Maria's Story: 1773, and *John's Story: 1775* were published in 2000 and 2001. They show life at different economic levels in the twenty-five years leading up to the American Revolution.[27]

Nixon discovered an unusual fact while reading about Williamsburg. Men who sailed with the pirate Blackbeard had been in prison there. All were hanged except the cabin boy. Local legend says that Blackbeard's ghost haunts the jail. Nixon thinks that's great![28]

CHAPTER 7

Fun and Facts

Can rib-tickling tall tales come from the woman who writes scary stories like *The Other Side of Dark* and *A Deadly Game of Magic*? Indeed they can. Joan Nixon loves to laugh, and she uses that humor in several books for younger readers.

She has long been known as the creator of strong female characters. The Shirley and Claude series features an irrepressible pioneer feminist and her companion. In the first book, *If You Say So, Claude*, Shirley and her husband Claude leave the noisy mining camps of Colorado in search of a quiet spot on the Texas frontier. They travel by covered wagon from one exciting adventure to another until they reach the perfect spot.

Fat Chance, Claude tells how independent-minded Shirley refused to marry dull Elmer Twaddle and went off to pan for gold. She meets Claude, whose only baby picture has a beard penciled in. He's convinced that "no purty woman like you would want to marry an ugly old coot like me." Shirley replies, "Turn you down? Fat chance, Claude."[1]

In *You Bet Your Britches, Claude,* the couple adopts a little boy and girl. *Beats Me, Claude* has Shirley warding off bad men with her apple pies. In *That's the Spirit, Claude*, Claude crawls on the roof to play "Sandy Claus" and meets the real Santa.

Nixon switched to a mystery for the younger crowd in 2000. Two savvy penguins star in *Gus and Gertie and the Missing Pearl*. The penguins vacation at a hotel where less-than-desirable characters are having a convention. Tourist Gus takes pictures. After Gertie's pearl

---

Can rib-tickling tall tales come from the woman who writes scary stories like *The Other Side of Dark* and *A Deadly Game of Magic?* Indeed they can.

---

necklace is stolen, Gus's snapshots reveal the culprit. Gus's camera again comes in handy in *Gus and Gertie and the Lucky Charms*. The pair hoped to win gold medals for synchronized swimming at the Animal Winter Olympics, but swimming competition is only for summer games. Instead, they chase bad guys over Olympic trails and catch the culprits who have stolen charms from the athletes.

On the opposite end of the scale from these light-hearted stories are several nonfiction books written with husband Hershell Nixon. These books are in his field of geology. He supplied the scientific knowledge for the six books. Her job was to make them easy for elementary age children to read.[2]

They began working together when Eileen asked questions about air pollution. Their first effort was called *What Is Your Weatherman Saying?* Unfortunately, the book never sold, but five other science books were published between 1977 and 1985. The National Science Teachers Association and Children's Book Council Joint Committee honored three of the books. *Volcanoes: Nature's Fireworks*; *Glaciers: Nature's Frozen Rivers*; and *Earthquakes: Nature in Motion* were chosen as Outstanding Science Trade Books for Children the years they were published.[3]

With Hershell Nixon's interest in geology, the couple visited Sedona, Arizona. They took a hot air balloon ride to view the unusual formations of beautiful red rocks. As they lifted off, she noticed a man placing something in the trunk of his car. Turning to her husband, she said, "Suppose he had just committed a crime and was stuffing the body bags in the trunk."

Her husband sighed. "Can't you just enjoy this lovely scenery and forget about mysteries for a while?"[4]

Apparently not.

CHAPTER 8

Consider the Children

With her vivid imagination Joan Lowery Nixon could have sat at her computer and continued to turn out award winning stories. But the "lady who is raring to go" believes in helping others.

About ten years ago, she was sent on a tour by her publisher. One of her first stops was at the Philadelphia Free Library. The Pennsylvania library holds special programs to help teen mothers learn parenting skills. As part of their program librarians show how to read a picture book to a child. Authors are invited to speak so that the mothers can meet someone who creates the stories.

Nixon looked around the room and wondered why she had been chosen to speak. Most of the young women had never read one of her books. Many of them probably could not read the books.

She was seated at a table with several young mothers

and their children. The mother next to her held a squirming eighteen-month-old. The child babbled the whole time. She wriggled out of her mother's arms, first climbing down, then climbing up. The mother had to watch constantly.

On the other side of Nixon a large girl had a tiny infant less than a month old. She turned to the first mother and said, "You wanna make 'em mind, you gotta whomp 'em."

The comment cut Nixon to the heart. "Oh," she thought, "her baby doesn't have a chance." Nixon gave her speech and went on to her next engagement, but she could not get the incident out of her mind. She had to find a way to show young parents that hitting is not the right way to discipline children.[1]

Thinking back on that day, she remembered how silent the room became while the librarian was reading the picture book. The short picture book appealed to the mothers. She knew that they would be turned off by a regular child care book. Maybe a picture book would get their attention.

Nixon began a whirlwind campaign to produce such a book. First, she turned to a *Houston Post* columnist who had written an article about children at risk. She called the reporter and said, "You don't know me, but I read your article. I want to write a picture book for girls who are teen moms, showing them how to take care of their babies. It should have photographs, not drawings. They can relate to photographs of girls and their babies. And I want to give it to them free. I don't know who to go to or where to get started."[2]

The man laughed and said he did know who she was. His children read her books. The reporter gave Nixon the name of someone to contact. That contact led to others. Eventually she got in touch with the

Mental Health Association of Greater Houston (Texas), an organization connected to several child care agencies.

Everyone was enthusiastic about the idea for preventing child abuse. Since the books were to be free, Nixon turned to friends, relatives, and charitable organizations to help with the cost. The graphics were donated. A printer promised to print 50,000 copies for free, with a minimum charge for an equal number of books. Nixon's Kappa Delta Sorority Foundation gave $15,000. Several years earlier Nixon had donated a story to *Ms.* Magazine. She contacted them, and the *Ms.* Magazine Foundation sent $4,000.[3]

Eileen McGowan pitched in to help her mother. McGowan supervised the photography of young mothers in parenting classes at a Houston high school. Each model received a copy of the book and an 8x10 copy of the photograph showing her with her baby.

Nixon crafted her words to let a mother tell how she cares for her baby. Each page ends like a lullaby— "Sweet little lovey baby. My baby."[4]

My Baby

"I'll never leave my baby alone....

"I keep my baby clean and dry....

"I never get mad at my baby for crying."[5]

My Baby was published in 1993 in English and very shortly after that in Spanish. Every mother who takes a newborn home from Ben Taub and the

Memorial Hospital System in Houston receives a copy of the book.

Five years later Nixon created *My Promise*. Nixon wanted to break the cycle of hitting that most of the mothers knew from their own childhood. This book, also free, shows healthy ways to discipline children. The voice of a young mother speaks about giving encouragement, using kind words, and setting fair rules. In the refrain the mother promises unconditional love no matter what the situation.[6]

Children's Protective Services in Houston helped finance the printing of *My Promise*. Kappa Delta was again involved in producing a book that is used by many agencies. Nurses and counselors for Head Start and the Houston Independent School District keep

My Promise

"It's hard to always do what's right,

but you and I can try to find the way.

Because I love you.

I'll always love you

and I'll do my best to help you

feel good about yourself. I promise.

Because I love you.

I'll always love you."[7]

copies in their offices. Shelters and counseling centers provide copies. Pediatricians place them in their waiting rooms. The Houston Public Library and the Houston Police Department Family Violence Unit distribute copies. Area schools receive copies each April during Child Abuse Prevention Month.[8]

Every year about 30,000 English-language copies and 40,000 copies in Spanish are given away. It is hard to know the exact number. Anyone who wishes to make copies is welcome to do so. The only restriction is that there can be no charge for the books nor any advertising placed in them.[9]

Terri Urbina, Children's Services Director with the Mental Health Association of Greater Houston, calls *My Baby* and *My Promise* "child abuse prevention tools in disguise." She received a letter from an inmate of a Texas prison. His wife had sent him a copy of *My Promise*. The man said it made him cry. The book made him realize that he was only repeating the abuse that his father had handed down to him. He was going to counseling to become a better father.[10]

Besides the books for young parents, Nixon also developed programs to promote literacy and reading. Nixon knew the power of mystery stories. While president of the Mystery Writers of America from May 1997 to May 1998, she started two ambitious programs.[11]

In the first one, Nixon worked with the Barnes & Noble bookstore in Houston. They organized a nationwide Kids Love a Mystery event. This became an annual affair held each February. It now involves bookstores and libraries nationwide. Through a website, http://www.kidsloveamystery.com, children have year-round access to puzzles and mini-mysteries. One section is devoted to Nancy Drew stories and another traces the history of mystery stories. Children

Joan pioneered several nationwide programs to get children excited about reading mysteries, and to help adults who have trouble reading.

earn an Eddie Award certificate by reading a mystery or by writing their own mystery. Nixon wrote instructions for teachers to show how to use mysteries in the classroom.[12]

The second project targeted adults who could not read difficult books. She asked the vice-president of NTC Contemporary Books in Chicago, Illinois, to publish books especially for this audience. "These adults don't want to read books written for young children. They need mysteries that are of interest to them, but in simpler language." He enthusiastically agreed, and Nixon put out a call for writers for the adult literacy project.[13]

Ten mystery writers worked on the Thumbprint

Series. Each author wrote three stories. One is fourth grade reading level, a second is sixth grade level, and a third is eighth grade level. For her own contribution Nixon paired with daughter Kathleen Brush. Their three books revolve around a character named Stacy Champagne.

Authors often get fan letters that say "Your book is the best book I ever read." The Thumbprint series brought another response. Canadian author Ellen Godfrey received an enthusiastic note from a reader. "That was the first book I ever finished. I loved it and want to read more." The series had done its work.[14]

Nixon no longer does school visits, but she has long been involved with young people's efforts at creative writing. It started in Corpus Christi when she volunteered to teach sessions on writing to eighth graders at St. Patrick's School. Her two older girls were in those classes. Nixon provided techniques to improve writing skills. Kathleen Brush appreciated the way her mother showed one aspect of writing at a time. "She would read examples of how various authors had created mood for their story, then give us time to try our hand at that."[15]

Maureen Quinlan saw long-lasting results of her mother's efforts. "Everyone looked forward to the days my mother came to teach creative writing. Mom would cover a topic: action words, exciting openings, sensory description. . . . We would write using our newly learned technique. . . . I could recognize the results of Mom's labors when my class took speech the next year."[16]

Nixon continues to share with students through the Internet. Both Random House and Scholastic feature her in their author section. On the Scholastic site Nixon posted ideas similar to the ones she used with her

Children were always important to Joan. In school visits, she offered encouragement to students to become the best that they could be.

daughters' classes. She gives instructions that a young person can follow in writing a mystery story.

A few years ago Nixon initiated a Girl Scout merit badge for writing. Her Kappa Delta Sorority had chosen the Girl Scouts as a service project. Patti Keplinger, president of the Houston Kappa Delta alumnae association at the time, searched for something other than cookie sales or troop sponsorship as a local project. Nixon proposed the Share a Story Project.[17]

To earn a Girl Scout Kappa Delta patch, the girls write and illustrate a story using helps Nixon created. After their stories are complete, they share the story with younger girls. In Houston, the stories are donated to Ben Taub Children's Ward and Children's Library.

The girls learn communication skills as they develop self esteem and concern for others.

The Share a Story Project is now nationwide, but it started in Houston, Texas. On Girl Scout Sunday 1998, the girls met to read their stories and receive badges. Nixon was there. She commented on each story and autographed any of her books that the girls had brought. Then the girls marched over to Ben Taub Hospital and presented their stories to the children's department.[18]

Patti Keplinger, who chaired many Kappa Delta charity events, summed it up. "She always responded as if she had all the time in the world for filling a request for help and seemed to enjoy sharing her talent."[19]

Chapter 9

The Gift of Reading

Joan Lowery Nixon died suddenly on June 28, 2003, of complications related to pancreatic cancer. During her life, she touched people in many ways. She was both humorous and compassionate. She placed great emphasis on her family but found time to be supportive of friends, writers, and young adults who contacted her.

In the Nixon family, grandchildren hold a special place. The mystery writer sometimes sent them letters written in lemon juice. The writing turned brown when heated over a light bulb. Eileen McGowan commented on her mother's dual nature, "She can plot a murder like a mastermind, yet treat her grandchildren with such tenderness."[1]

McGowan got a taste of her mother's sense of humor when they worked together on an anthology called *Mother & Daughters: Celebrating the Gift of Love With 12 New Stories*. Their contribution, "Try to

Survive," was inspired by three-year-old Katie. Katie had hidden her shoes. Nixon laughed and said, "What goes around comes around." McGowan protested that she was never like that. Nixon replied, "You were worse!" How then had her mother survived *three* daughters? Nixon laughed again. "The same way you will."[2]

Even though she was a grandmother, Nixon was not above a prank herself. One evening she organized a sleep-over for some of her Houston friends. The women put on their pajamas and watched Humphrey Bogart in the classic movie *Casablanca*. Each time Bogart appeared they pretended to swoon. After the movie was over, they decided to "wrap" the house of a friend who could not come that night. They giggled over what they would say if a policeman caught them throwing the rolls of toilet paper into the trees. But they were too tired to carry out the project. The next day they called the friend to tell her about their failed plan. She replied, "You should've left the toilet paper on my porch with a note! I'd have done it myself!"[3]

Nixon loves to tell stories of herself, like the one involving her son Joe. He is a lawyer and a member of the Texas legislature. One evening he was in the shower when his sixth grade son received a phone call. Nicholas kept coming in to ask questions about his grandmother. After several exchanges, Joe Nixon took the phone. The girl had a report due the next day. He answered a few more questions and asked if she needed anything else. "No," replied the girl, "I think I've got three minutes' worth here."[4]

Joan and Hershell Nixon also played a large part in the lives of twelve children in Burma and India. Over the course of thirty-five years, they sponsored children through the Foster Parent Mission, a Catholic agency. Their first foster child was named Carmel. She was twelve years old at the time, the same age as Maureen. The Nixons have put two of the children through college. Pictures of all of the foster children were on the office wall facing Nixon as she wrote each day.[5]

Writer Mary Blount Christian spoke fervently about Nixon's personal concern for others. "When I was injured or ill, she was the first at my door with meals and offers to run errands or anything to help, despite her

Writing Is. . .

"Writing is a complicated mixture of talent, art, craft, structure, free flowing ideas, unleashed imagination, soaring hopes, wondrous insights, giddy joy, deep satisfaction, dreadful insecurity, total misery, strong persistence, and solid determination."[6]

busy schedule and many obligations. She is an incredible friend and I [celebrated] each day, knowing her."[7]

Nixon shrugged off discussion of her own bout with cancer. She did not think anyone would find the subject interesting. "I arranged appearances in between [chemotherapy] sessions," she once said. "I feel that having books to work on and appearances to make kept my mind off the bad part."[8]

Nixon was especially encouraging to authors of children's books. For several years she taught overflowing creative writing classes in the evening at the University of Houston. Each session presented clear writing guidelines for a particular type of children's literature.[9]

She became a founding member of the Society of Children's Book Writers and Illustrators (SCBWI) when it was organized in Los Angeles, California,

Joan and Hershell celebrated their 50th wedding anniversary in 1999.

more than thirty years ago. She continued to support the Houston chapter of SCBWI by participating in writing conferences, programs, and workshops. In 2000 she volunteered to mentor the author of the most promising manuscript submitted at the annual Houston SCBWI conference. Dede Ducharme, recent recipient, said, "Joan [was] at the top of my list of word wizards. Her suggestions were so amazing. . . what a difference good editorial suggestions can make."[10]

Nixon was especially pleased to hear from young people. She received about one hundred e-mails and letters a week. Letters awaiting answers were stacked beside her computer. Kids eagerly told her how much they liked her books. Some letters poured out stories of abuse. Nixon became a surrogate mother and tried to give comfort.

Hershell Nixon was his wife's most devoted fan. He knew why kids wanted to talk to her. "It's because her writing gives them a feeling of hope. Through her heroines, she tells children that anything is possible for them. 'Be strong, be confident. You can do things.'"[11]

One reluctant reader summed up the joy she found in Joan Lowery Nixon's books. "Thanks for the gift of reading."[12]

When Joan Lowery Nixon died, her fans assumed that *Nightmare*, the manuscript scheduled for release by Delacorte Press, would be the last mystery from this prolific author. They were wrong.

Nixon had been working on another middle-grade mystery. This time, her grandson, Matt Nixon, was the moving force. Matt had taken a stand-up comedy class taught by a comedian who is also a Houston policeman. "We had this thing at some of the night clubs last summer, where all the kids do stand-up jokes. My grandmother came to see it." And, of course, she was off and running with another story idea.

Matt, now a seasoned joke teller, was not shy about supplying jokes to his grandmother. "She had . . . really lame [jokes] . . . so I gave her some [good ones]." It was a business deal. Matt was paid $5 a joke.[13]

Before the book was completed, however, Nixon's final illness intervened. She was scheduled to enter the hospital mid-May for an operation. On the Sunday before her surgery, she stayed at her computer all day finishing *Laugh Until You Cry*.

This last act summed up the things that defined Joan Lowery Nixon. It speaks eloquently of her work ethic. The genre was mystery, her specialty. The woman who loved to laugh incorporated jokes into the story. And above all, this last book, dedicated to her grandson Matt, involved her family.

Joan Lowery Nixon left a rich legacy for everyone— family, friends, and admirers.

In Her Own Words

Interviewer: Mary Dodson Wade, at the Nixon home, Houston, TX, September 26, 2002

MDW: You grew up in California. I believe you have two sisters.

JLN: Yes, my sister Pat—Patricia Lowery Collins—lives in Massachusetts. She has eight paperbacks and two young adult books. She is a poet and an artist. One of her paintings is in the New Hampshire statehouse.

My sister Marilyn writes romance, and she has a book on how to write romances.

MDW: Your mother was a kindergarten teacher. She seemed to encourage your creativity.

JLN: Yes, when we were young, we had a playroom that was filled with things to encourage us to express ourselves. We had clay we could mold. We had colors and could draw and create pictures. She wanted to be a model mother and belonged to a woman's group that shared ideas on how to raise children.

MDW: It sounds very Montessori.

JLN: Oh, yes. Her kindergarten was a Montessori kindergarten.

My grandparents lived in the other part of the house. My grandfather was retired, and he read to me.

I got an interesting video the other day. I had been told that I was in a Fox Movietone Film because I could read when I was three. The video place was restoring some of the old films before they disintegrated. This included out-takes from the film that was shown in movie theaters. They couldn't locate the film, but an editor saw the child's name, Joan Lowery, and thought maybe it was a children's writer named Joan Lowery Nixon. They sent me a copy. My granddaughter thought it was very funny to watch her Grandma.

MDW: I have heard you say on several occasions that you thought of a poem and would go to your mother and say, "Mama, write it down."

JLN: I was writing before I was knew how to write the letters. But, I was a rowdy child too. We used to have weed fights, especially when the ground was soft after a rain. It was safe then, and we loved to play out until dark. We had a game called First Light. The first person to see the street light got to tag all the others.

I loved to roller skate. Our house was on the corner. All the driveways were long and sloping. I would start down our driveway and up the neighbor's drive and keep going. I could get up pretty good speed.

MDW: Your mother kept a scrapbook.

JLN: Yes, I was the oldest child, so my scrapbook was quite large. My sisters didn't have as many pictures in theirs. The scrapbook ended when I was about eight or nine, but later I added things myself.

MDW: Do you think growing up in Hollywood affected your life as a writer?

JLN: I'm not sure that it did, but it certainly was a place to have unusual experiences. As a teen, I rode the streetcar to school. Walking up the hill one day, I met a person dressed in a gorilla suit handing out business cards. Where else would you find a gorilla handing out business cards?

I got to go to Frank Sinatra's radio show. I didn't scream, though. I thought that was silly. I'm not sure they didn't pay the girls to scream.

Many of my schoolmates were in the movies. Someone would disappear and not be back for the rest of the year because they had parts in a film. They were taught on the set. But we had the best school plays because of all of these out-of-work actors. Everyone took drama classes.

MDW: Your friend Mary Lou...

JLN: Mary Lou and I are still friends. We used to go on the street car to the beach. Looking at it now, that was a long way, but we loved it.

MDW: Your first publication was at age 10.

JLN: Yes, it was a children's magazine that had a page of children's writing. My poem was called "Springtime." It had my byline, and said age 10. I wrote lots of poems for relatives. I made greeting cards for my grandparents.

MDW: I understand that in high school you wrote poems that other girls sent to servicemen.

JLN: Yes.

MDW: Your first sale...

JLN: It was to *Ford Times*. I looked at a copy and thought I could write that kind of article. I told about how to entertain children on trips. I was 17. I pretended I was my mother. I believe I was paid $35.

MDW: You majored in journalism in college.

JLN: I started college one week after I graduated from Hollywood High School. I was 17. It was during the war, and the University of Southern California trained officers for the Navy and Marines. They had three semesters a year so the officers could finish as quickly as possible. That's why I could start so soon.

As one of my assignments, I was on the staff of a fan

magazine called "Hollywood Entertainers." My job was to interview starlets, not the big name stars because I was so young. I could not drive so I would go across the street to the frat house to get one of the boys to drive me. They were more than willing to take me to interview starlets. I remember one starlet was very glamorous. She had on a dress that was slit down to her navel. It had mesh but you couldn't see that until you were close up. I don't remember her name. But one of the starlets who became famous was Cyd Charisse.

MDW: Your father was opposed to journalism.

JLN: Yes, he was always being interviewed by newspaper reporters. He thought they were a rough crowd, and he didn't want me to associate with them. They drank a lot. I didn't want to drink. I didn't want to be a newspaper reporter. I wanted to be a war correspondent. Of course, the war was over by the time I graduated.

MDW: How did journalism affect your writing career?

JLN: First, it taught me to do research. That was useful in writing nonfiction. It taught me organization of material. It also taught me to think on a typewriter. We even had to take tests on a typewriter. Creative writing is different, but even in fiction you need to explain Who, What, When, Where, and How. And it teaches you to apply the seat of the pants to the chair and work even if inspiration doesn't strike. I had a teacher argue with me when I said that to students. She felt that creative writing only came with inspiration. I feel that if you work, the inspiration will come.

MDW: You also taught kindergarten for a while like your mother.

JLN: There was a great need for teachers. I had not had any education courses. I substituted for the first semester, then took the job full-time. There were two rooms of kindergartners. The other teacher was very good. I watched what she did. We were right across from the California State College and I would leave school and go over there for night classes. I taught three years.

MDW: How did you and Nick meet?

JLN: Friends fixed us up. It wasn't really a blind date. I knew who he was, but I thought he was going with someone else. The friends said they thought he had broken up with the girl.

MDW: Nick is a geologist, and you have lived in several different places with his work.

JLN: Nick first worked for Shell. We were in Billings, Montana. For three years, he was out in the field during the summer. Because the men were gone all summer, they were encouraged to take their families. We had Kathy, so she and I went along. Western Montana is beautiful. We stayed in this little motel. It had no kitchen. There was one cafe where everyone ate, and all they served was steak and potatoes. One day I asked if they didn't have a salad. "Oh, yes," the waitress answered. She brought me potato salad.

We lived in Palmdale, California, where they built the huge airfield. Then he worked for Tidewater, and we lived in Ventura, California. Later, we were in San Francisco and then back in Los Angeles. We came to Texas in the early 1960s. We lived in Corpus Christi, Houston, went to Midland, and then came back to Houston and have been here ever since. Nick worked with Mitchell Energy until he retired.

MDW: Where were the children born?

JLN: Well, Kathy was born in Los Angeles. Maureen was too because Nick was sent to Houston for a three-month project, so I came back to Los Angeles for her to be born. Joe was born in Ventura, and Eileen in San Mateo.

MDW: Did any of the places you've lived make it into a book?

JLN: Not really. But many years later I wrote *Ghost*

Town. It is a collection of ghost stories set in different places. One of them is about Maiden, Montana. I met one of the founders of Maiden. He bought the whole town. He was the only one living there, and I interviewed him. But the story is fiction.

There was not much to do during the summers. Sometimes Kathy and I rode in the back seat when the geologists went out. That was before the days of air-conditioning, and we rolled down the car windows. The trouble was that they were having a grasshopper invasion. The grasshoppers were flying in the windows. Kathy was screaming, and I was fighting grasshoppers. The other geologist threatened to make us stay in the motel.

While we were there, Kathy broke out in a red rash. Then someone told us that the government had condemned the water. We drove for miles to get water to drink.

MDW: You and Nick have had some health problems. You kept working.

JLN: Yes, but the subject is not something that I think would be interesting for a book. For a year I wore the chemo pump for two weeks and then would be off for two weeks. I arranged appearances in between sessions. I feel that having books to work on and appearances to make kept my mind off the bad part.

MDW: You wrote some books with Nick.

JLN: We worked together on several science books—glaciers, volcanoes, earthquakes, and the land under the sea.

MDW: You have 13 grandchildren. Are any of them in your books?

JLN: Melia and Nikki are in the Nic-Nak Neighborhood series. Brian and Sean are in the Casebuster books.

MDW: You have membership in a number of professional organizations.

JLN: I'm a member of Mystery Writers of America. I won the Edgar four times. I belong to the Authors' Guild and the Society of Children's Book Writers and Illustrators. I'm also member of the Western Writers of America and Women Writing the West. I also belong to Sisters in Crime.

MDW: You were president of Mystery Writers of America. I know that you wanted to do something more than just have a title. Tell me about the programs you started.

JLN: One was "Kids Love a Mystery." It began here in Houston. The Barnes & Noble bookstore coordinator liked the idea and brought in the New York office. They picked up the tab for the event. Mystery writers across the nation appeared at Barnes & Noble. There was a writing part too, and those who participated got certificates. There were lots of different activities, art, and puzzles. The program is still going on.

The other program helped adults learn to read. We put out a call for ten mystery writers to write three books each. The first would be easy to read, the next one harder, and the third one still harder. I worked with Kathy on the Champagne books.

MDW: Your historical books include the Orphan Train Adventure books. How did you get the idea for that series?

JLN: My agent's husband is a packager. He called and said, "I'd like for you to read this article about the Orphan Train children." He told his wife this would make a wonderful series but who would write it? They both said at the same time "Joan Nixon." I read the article when it came and called him up and said, "I have got to write these books. This is just very, very moving."

I read whatever I could find about the orphan train children, which was very little. I went to New York and met with the people at the Children's Aid Society. They were very helpful. They gave me some of the original journals from the 1800s. They were covered in blue paper, and they were so old they cracked. They had a collection of letters from the agents, from the kids.

Then I had to write what is called the bible— everything I could think of about the story, about how it would be put together, who the characters would be. I invented the family, the time, the place. I put this all together and sent it to him. He had me come back up to New York and talk to some editors about it.

I wrote the synopsis of the first four books. My agent sent it to about a dozen publishers. They bid for the right to publish the series. Bantam wanted it badly. The editor there just loved the idea. We did four books, and later she let me write two more. Then she called me one day and said, "Why don't you write one that sums it all up? Have Frances Mary be grown up and then we'll do a spin-off into Orphan Train Children." So we did four books about some children who were on the orphan train that Frances Mary was chaperoning.

It's really nice that the Orphan Train riders have gotten some recognition. In Iowa the state devoted a whole program to their Orphan Train riders based on what they had learned in my books, and they had a statewide celebration for these people. Many of the schools use them as classroom sets. They study this as part of history now.

MDW: You attended a meeting of the organization.

JLN: The society is headquartered in Springdale, Arkansas. They have a museum and have a national convention there every October. Then they have statewide conventions.

MDW: I've heard you mention the wonderful ladies that came to the Texas Book Festival. (A book festival that features authors speaking about their books. The festival was started in Austin, TX, while Laura Bush was First Lady of Texas.)

JLN: They were wonderful. I set the thing up through

their daughters. The mothers were very excited about coming. I told the daughters that I would make sure they were invited to the [governor's] mansion for a buffet breakfast that Laura Bush always gave for the writers. George W. Bush, the governor, was there too. One woman said, "Little ole me. That's going to be the most important day of my life."

Well, they met the governor, and bless his heart, I went in and told him, "There are two orphan train riders here who want to meet you," and then quickly told him what an orphan train rider was. And, this is so typical of George W. Bush, he didn't say, "Bring them to me." He said, "Lead me to them." And so, I was taking him out of the dining room as they came in. And he fussed over them, and he put his arms around them. He kissed one on the forehead. He posed for as many pictures as they wanted. He was just wonderful. They were so excited.

So then they were in the parlor, and Nick came in and said, "Former President Bush has just come in, would they like to meet him?" They both just jumped to their feet, and I took them in and introduced them. He was every bit as gracious as George W. Bush was. They were so thrilled.

The festival has talks all over the state capitol. Former President Bush spoke about his book. I had arranged for them to sit in legislators' chairs so they could have a good view of everything. I was up in the balcony watching them having fun. Our talk was scheduled next in a different room. It was packed. We had people sitting on the floor. Everyone wanted to hear these women, and so I really didn't say much about my book, just "Here's my book about the orphan train, now let's hear what these orphan train riders have to say."

One woman held up a little coat, about a size 18-months, and she said, "This is the coat I wore when I was on the orphan train." Some of the audience began to cry. You could hear this, "Ohhhh."

Somebody asked her in the question period that followed, "Did they make you work hard?" And she said, "Yes. . . but everybody worked hard. We lived on a farm. We all worked hard." Then she said, "If they made the kids today work as hard as we did, they wouldn't be in all this trouble." She got a round of applause for that. They were delightful.

There is a fellow named Art Smith, who is very active in going out and speaking about his experiences as an orphan train rider. All he knows about his past is that he was found in a little box under a dress rack in Gimbels Department Store. He knows nothing at all about his mother, his father, where he came from. It's very interesting, some of their stories.

MDW: You also have the Ellis Island series.

JLN: That's out of print now, unfortunately. I do get lots of good letters about it. The kids like it, and the teachers like it.

MDW: How did you get the idea?

JLN: My editor called me and said, "You told me that three of your grandparents came to this country from other countries. Would you like to write a book about three girls who come to the United States through Ellis Island?" She wanted them to meet on the boat.

I told her I was interested. She had a request. "I'd like the first girl to be Jewish. I don't care what country you have her come from, and I want them to settle in the garment district in New York. Make the second girl Irish because two of your grandparents came from Ireland." I said, "Well, I think I'd have them go to Chicago." And she said, "You choose the third one."

We had talked about the 1800s. I began reading about Ellis Island. It was very corrupt at that time, but [President] Teddy Roosevelt sent a friend to clean up the place. I called my editor and said, "Let's make it 1902 or later because we don't want the corruption to interfere with the immigration experience." She agreed with me.

I said, "I'm going to have the first girl come from Russia because they are coming to save their lives. And the second family is going to come one at a time. The father comes first, and then he works to bring the next one. The mother and the two younger children are still in Ireland when Rosie comes over. They come to keep from starving to death. I want the third girl to come from Sweden because Sweden is very socialistic. You couldn't buy land, so they come to get farm land. I'll put them in Minnesota." She said that was fine, just get busy on the books.

MDW: The Williamsburg series, the idea and the research for that....

JLN: The editor of publications at Colonial Williamsburg had read the Orphan Train books. She contacted the packager for the Orphan Train series. I agreed to write the books if the same publisher could publish them.

The people at Colonial Williamsburg had a definite number in mind, six books. They had worked out the idea of who the children would be. I made one change because they had four boys and two girls. I said, "Let's have three and three." I picked a girl who would be the right age, and the right situation, one with a different economic condition.

I worked with the historians. The historians had no knowledge about book schedules. Sometimes this made it difficult for the editors because the editors couldn't get what they needed in time to fit the publication schedule. The historians took so long because they read the manuscript only on such and such a day, that sort of thing. But they were very, very helpful. It wasn't just one historian reading a manuscript. Every historian was involved. One historian was in charge of food, another in charge of clothing. Whatever entered into that book, they had that expert check it out. Everything in those books is totally, totally accurate. And that part I like. It was very good.

MDW: You went to Williamsburg.

JLN: I spent a week in Williamsburg with a historian constantly at my side, taking me to everything, showing me everything. I even went to some of the programs they were doing for kids. I took in a tremendous amount of material. They had sent me a huge box full of books to read before I went. Then they sent me another box after we had an editorial meeting there. And then, of course, I could use their website. All I had to do was call the editor and say, "I need to know such and such" and they would find it for me. Different questions would arise. Like when I was writing about Will, his father is the jailor as well as the organist for the church, I said, "Do you have any record of the prisoners who were in the jail at this particular time and what happened to them?" Well, they did. They made a list of the prisoners and their convictions or acquittals.

One of the things intrigued me. There was a man there named Miles Mansfield, and he had committed a felony. The punishment for a felony was hanging. He had been a clerk for a man who wouldn't pay him, so he wrote himself a check for the amount that was owed to him. And this was considered stealing. But he was not hanged. He was given a whipping, and I wanted to know why. He did something to merit this lesser punishment, so what am I going to have him do? I made it up. There was a slave there in the prison too, a runaway, and he wouldn't tell who his master was. He escaped. So there were different things I could put together.

In reading I found out that Blackbeard's men had been in the prison. They had all been hanged, except the cabin boy. Some people claimed that Blackbeard haunted the prison. That was just great as far as I was concerned!

They gave me a lot of good material. I put things together, and then I would say to them, "OK, who would his best friend have been?" Then they would come back and say, "Well, So-and-So lived very close and they were the same age. These people were in the same economic strata. They probably hung out together. " This is how I got friends. These are all real people too.

MDW: Did you change the names?

JLN: No, no, they were real persons. I tried to make it as close to their lives as possible. There's no way in the world to know what two little boys would have talked about, but there is a way of guessing that they probably would have. . . so you can do it that way.

MDW: And did you put historical figures in there?

JLN: Oh yes, George Washington is in there on occasion, and Thomas Jefferson most definitely. There were others in there. One was the father of the boy in the sixth book. He was the treasurer of the Virginia Commonwealth. He was very conservative. He was very much against what Britain was doing, but he wanted to work it out, talk about it, to negotiate. Well, his oldest son was a real hothead. He led a group into the governor's palace and robbed the guns there. He was quite a hothead and his father was very conservative. Here is the younger brother. Who would he have sided with—his brother or his father? He would have been torn between the two ideas. That gave me quite a bit to go on.

MDW: You also have books about what I call social issues, the one about not hitting children.

JLN: Delacorte sent me on a book tour. At the first stop I thought it was an odd place, but I see that there was a reason for my being there. It was the Philadelphia Free Library. They have a program every year for teen mothers and their children, their babies. The library staff serves cookies and punch, and they try to teach the girls something about taking care of their children. They talk to them about reading to their children. One librarian showed how to read a picture book. I still don't know why they decided to put me on this program. Very few of those mothers could have read one of my books.

I was seated with them until it was my turn to talk. The young girl next to me had a little child about 18-months old that would climb on her lap and climb down and babble a little bit, the way babies do. And the girl on the other side, very heavyset girl, had a brand new baby. The baby was about two weeks old. She turned to this girl and said, "You wanna make 'em mind, you gotta whomp 'em."

I was thinking, "Oh, her baby doesn't have a chance." It disturbed me so much. That was my first stop on the tour, but I kept thinking about these girls. They had no attention span. They were very interested, though, when the librarian read the picture book. I thought, "If I put a childcare book into their hands, they wouldn't read it, but if it was a picture book, they might get something out of it."

The more I thought about it, the more I knew that this was something I wanted to do. The babies are here. Now what are we going to do about it? I called a fellow who wrote a column in the *Post* [Houston newspaper that has ceased publication]. He had written about children at risk. So I called the reporter and said, "You don't know me, but I read your article. I want to write a picture book for girls who are teen moms showing them how to take care of their babies. It should have photographs, not drawings. They can relate to photographs of girls and their babies. And I want to give it to them free. I don't know who to go to, or where to get started."

He said, "I know who you are. My children read your books. I think this is a great idea." He sent me to one person and that person sent me to another. We ended up eventually with the Mental Health Association. We had a board to give me some direction. It is made up of representatives of different child care agencies in Houston.

The only trouble was we had to get the money so that the book could be given free. Many of these young mothers couldn't buy the book, but they would read it probably if it was put in their hands. Somebody said, "Don't worry about the money. The money will come." And I thought, "OK, we'll see what we can do." I called on everybody I knew. I called my cousin and said, "Do you mind if I call your fiancé. He owns a graphics company here." Well, he said they would do the graphics for free. He knew a printer. The printer said, "I'll give you the first 50,000 copies free and charge a minimum for the second 50,000." So we decided on a printing of 100,000.

My daughter Eileen said, "I'll supervise the photography. One of my friends is a photographer. She can take the pictures." I wrote to everybody. I had donated a story to *Ms.* magazine, and so I wrote to them and said, "I did this for you, now can you do this for me?" The *Ms.* Foundation sent $4000. I checked with my sorority foundation, and they said, "We'll give you $15,000." And it went on from there. We earned enough money, and with the free work, we printed 100,000 copies of *My Baby*. Then we raised money to get some of them done in Spanish.

They also asked me to do one about discipline. *My Promise* is in English and Spanish. We have given out so many. Every layette that goes to Ben Taub [Harris County hospital in Houston, Texas] has one of the books in English or Spanish, depending on the mother's language. The police carry the books in the car. If they go into a family disturbance call, and they feel one of the books is useful, they give the family a copy in English or Spanish. Doctors use them, the hospitals, schools that have parenting classes use them.

We used the girls in the parenting classes in Spring Branch [Houston suburban school district] as our models for our first book.

MDW: How did you get the photo releases?

JLN: We promised them a copy of the book and an 8x10 picture of them with their babies. They all agreed, so we got written permission. With the second book, we used children. Many of them were at this school near my house, or friends' children. We had to get releases for all them.

The daughter of the fellow who has the graphics company did the graphics for us. She said she lives by the book herself. She had two babies. It's been wonderful.

Anybody has permission to reprint the book as long as they do not charge for it and they don't put advertising in the book. A number of places have asked for permission to print copies. We don't really know who's doing it all, but it's reaching a lot of people. It's basic help.

I wrote the *My Baby* book from the viewpoint of a teen mom—this is what I do with my baby because you don't preach to a teenager. If I said, "Now, this is what you're supposed to do with your baby," their backs would go up. But if I say, "This is what I'm doing with my baby," or "I do not leave my baby to run down to the corner and get a coke". . . basic things that a lot of these girls don't think about because they are young.

MDW: The My Promise book. . .

JLN: *My Promise* is meant to break what they have known as discipline, which is Yell and Hit. Most of them, that's all they have known in their own lives. It shows them how you relate to your child, how you teach a child. Both books are doing well. The Child Protective Services gave us some money for the second book. We've had different foundations around Texas doing it. A wonderful woman who wanted to help anybody who speaks Spanish picked up the tab on that book in Spanish. So we just have great help. They tell me we're about to run out of books. I'll have to start fund raising. That's the tough part. I hate to go out and ask people for money, but they are very good about it.

MDW: The humorous books. . . my favorite are the books about Claude. Are those still available in paperback?

JLN: No. I'm sorry. All the Shirley and Claude books are out of print.

MDW: In the first one they are moving across Texas.

JLN: Looking for the perfect place to live.

MDW: It had such a wonderful local feeling for me. But your Gus and Gertie book is something different. I think I heard you say that book started out as something else and was morphed into the penguins.

JLN: Yes, I was going to use walruses at first and then decided on penguins. There are two Gus and Gertie books.

MDW: You work with several publishers. Is that simply because your agent sold to different publishers. You have mysteries with two publishers.

JLN: Well, right now I don't do a mystery for anybody except Random House. And the same thing with historical. I was asked to do a book for the Dear America series, and I didn't because my editor wanted me to stick with Random House. . . and I love working with her.

However, before I was working with her so closely, I did some mysteries with Scholastic. And one of them came back with a vengeance. I mean, everybody was asking for *The House on Hackman's Hill*, and it was out of print. I had a teacher who wanted 350 copies for their school district. It's a great book to start out with in September to get fifth graders hooked on reading. It's a scary book. Kids love it, and they immediately want to go to the library and get another scary book.

MDW: Was that the one based on your parents having visited a house?

JLN: No, this one has mummies in it, based on a visit to the Los Angeles county museum and getting scared of the mummies. My agent asked for the rights back, but Scholastic decided to reprint it. So they did, and it had a phenomenal sale. Of course, it's companion, *Haunted Island*, is out of print. If they'd bring that back into print, they would sell a lot of those.

MDW: I want to go back to your writing style itself. Some people keep journals. Do you keep a journal?

JLN: No.

MDW: But you do keep files for ideas. Tell me how you organize those.

JLN: I have a pocket file, and it's just labeled "Ideas." It's stuffed with newspaper clippings, scraps of paper. On some I've written more about what the book should be. It is all kinds of odds and ends that make me think, "I could use this in a mystery." For instance, I read newspapers wherever I go. One time there was an article about people who bought houses in which murders had taken place and didn't know it. Apparently the realtor does not have to tell you this. I clipped that out and stuck that in the folder and used that in my book *Whispers from the Dead*.

In the same book, I used an article I'd read about someone in Los Angeles who was with the psychology department at UCLA [University of California at Los Angeles]. They were interviewing teenagers and children who survived near-death experiences. They found that every one of them was in a state for two or three months in which they felt that there was some presence with them. It was not scary—it was comforting. It was as though they still had not quite left the next world they almost went into. I utilized that in *Whispers from the Dead*.

I never know when I'm going to use one of these things. I just have them in that file.

MDW: How do you go back to that file?

JLN: Oh, every once in a while I just dump it all out on the bed and start going through all these scraps of paper. Then I think, "Well. . . I can use this." Or somebody will say, "Can you write a story for this collection we're doing?" I'll dump it out and think, "This is not enough for a book, but it would be good for a story." It just refreshes my mind. I think, "Gosh, I forgot all about this," but, you know, I have it in there, so I've kept it.

MDW: Your book The Other Side of Dark was made into a TV movie.

JLN: It was a Monday Night Movie, on NBC.

MDW: Did you have any input at all in that?

JLN: The producer asked me if I'd like a copy of the script, and I said yes, so she sent me a copy. I called her up and said, "You know, there are some real holes in that script but I see how they could be fixed." She said, "It's already been filmed. We don't worry about holes in the script. We figured it was just holes in the mystery." She told me that the first writer read the book. The second script writer read the first script. The next person read that script. There were twenty rewrites.

MDW: Each generation took it farther away from the book.

JLN: I'm sure the star had a lot to do with it too. And it had really foolish stuff in it.

MDW: I understand that you did not care for the ending.

JLN: Well, I write about strong girls. They may not be the brightest in their class but they've got good common sense. And they may be scared to death, but they do something about it. And they are not going to go screaming, "Help! Help! Help!" They're going to think of what they're going to do to save themselves. And so in this case, the character is going, "Oooh, help, help, help." Somebody rushes in and helps her. So they lost the whole point of that. It would have been a much stronger ending if they had kept to the book.

And there were just foolish things, like at one place they were going swimming in this indoor pool. The only other person who knows she is going to be there is the boy she likes. And, you see somebody monkeying with the electric wires. There is no reason at all why somebody else knows that she is going to be there. She is tripping along in her little two-piece bathing suit. She's holding on to the metal railing. She puts her toe in the water. The screen goes blank, and then you see her in the doctor's office getting her toe bandaged because she got electrocuted. Now. . . [laugh] that is just too foolish.

MDW: Your memberships in particular organizations, how do you see that for a beginning writer? What do you recommend?

JLN: I recommend anybody who is going to write for children to join SCBWI [Society of Children's Book Writers and Illustrators]. It's a tremendous help. Their bulletin is full of good material. They have good marketing information. Their workshops and their conferences are tremendous help. When I started writing, I had one book to go by. It was written by Phyllis Whitney. A librarian gave it to me. . . no courses, no anything about writing for children. . . I just had Phyllis Whitney's book. And so now, I think, "Oh, if these people would just take advantage of these opportunities." Unfortunately, there are so many people who think I just sit down and write a book. They don't realize there are rules to learn. There are certain things you need to know about length, how to develop character, things they don't think about. Writing is tough. . . it's very tough. SCBWI is a great help to the people who belong. Some of the other organizations provide companionship from fellow writers. And the Author's Guild is wonderful.

[These comments occur while looking at the scrapbook.]

JLN: This was the car that belonged to Adolph Menjou. It was like a limousine, and the glass rolled up between the front and the back.

MDW: And when you got rowdy in the back, your mother rolled up the glass.

JLN: But it had jump seats so that we had enough seats for everybody.

MDW: You are in an Indian costume right there. Is that the one you made?

JLN: Yeah, that's my Indian costume. I cut the fringe. She [mother] helped me sew beads on it. And here are pictures of the Los Angeles earthquake. I think they are so interesting. This was the worst area in there, and we were right up in here.

You know there is the funniest thing. A few years ago when they had the big San Francisco quake. . . when was that. . 1988?. . . I was sent out there for a book tour. I was going to schools. I said to Nick, "San Francisco is going to have an earthquake." I took the big flashlight when I went to the hotel. I told them I'd like to be on one of the lower floors. I even had mapped out how I was going to get out of the city to the water because I thought they would take people out by boat. That's how much I felt this. The earthquake was a week after I came home. So, I mean, that was the strangest thing.

Here's what I wrote my father on my seventh birthday. "Boy, am I big. I'm seven years old, but I never saw in my life a Daddy so good as my Daddy is. He's just as good as gold."

So I was writing things. In fact, I'd write anything for anybody. My father had to give a speech when I was in high school. He said, "Can you write me a poem on victory gardens? So I wrote him a poem for his speech. My mother was on the program for the

Cornelia Club. She said, "I have to speak about adolescent girls, and there is no way in the world that I understand adolescent girls." I said, "Don't worry about it. I'll write your speech for you." So I did, and she gave it too.

MDW: In high school you were writing poems for girls to send off in the letters to the servicemen.

JLN: This is a story by Joan. How old was I? Nine. My mother typed it up. It's called "A Trip to Fairyland." [laugh]

This is one my family has always teased me about. My mother had asked us what we were going to be when we grew up. Marilyn said she was going to be a plain mother. And Joan spoke up and said, "Oh, I'm going to be a lady that's raring to go." [laugh] And my family said, "You said you were going to be a lady that was raring to go, and you never stopped."

MDW: (Those are) your puppets. I believe that picture is in The Making of a Writer.

JLN: No, I think it's another one.

MDW: That one would be a good one to have in the book.

JLN: Oh, here is my poem. It says age ten. It's called "Springtime."

The others are when I was in the seventh and eighth grade.

Now this is something I didn't even remember. This was so unusual. It's a little thumbnail sketch of me. It tells about our puppet show and says, "however Joan doesn't plan on making puppeteering her life career. Her great ambition is to write children's books and later to become a kindergarten teacher."

MDW: Did your mother add that part at the end? She was a kindergarten teacher.

JLN: No, apparently that's what I wanted to be—a kindergarten teacher.

MDW: And you were how old then?

JLN: Well, let's see, 1940, I was thirteen. No, it was my teacher in high school who told me to major in journalism. She insisted on it.

Oh, look, here's the name. . . *Children's Activities* [magazine containing "Springtime" poem]. It says, "Several of her stories and poems have been published in the magazine *Children's Activities*. I didn't notice that when I wrote my own book. [laugh]

MDW: So, by the time you were thirteen, you already knew you wanted to be a writer.

JLN: I knew that from the time I was born. I wrote and wrote and wrote and wrote.

Oh, here is the girls' drill team at Hollywood High.

MDW: What is this story in Making of a Writer about your having to wear an extra dress?

JLN: I had to wear a blanket under all this. It was very tight to get it on. I felt like I was just stuffed in it.

But this is the girl who looked like me, and here, I'm back here.

MDW: The fellow who was watching. . .

JLN: Yeah, he thought that was me.

And when I graduated my father took pictures. We were in the Hollywood Bowl. He took pictures of her, instead of me. [laugh] You can't tell so much, she really did look like me. We were both tall and had dark hair and wore our hair the same way.

Oh, that's a map of Hollywood High School campus. It's a big school. Look at all the buildings.

MDW: Oh my goodness, how did you keep from getting lost?

JLN: Well, it wasn't that. It was getting from one class to another. You had to scurry.

That's Mary Lou.

These are my two little sisters.

Oh, this is interesting. This is W.C. Fields' house. One time Mary Lou and I sneaked onto his lawn, and these are all taken at his house. Then that was all subdivided.

MDW: I don't remember when he died. Was he living there then?

JLN: Oh, yes, he was there at that time. I didn't like him because he was drunk a lot, and he had a real foul mouth. If I walked past his house, and I liked to walk up the hill, and if he was out there, he would yell things at me. He was just a disagreeable person.

Cecil B. DeMille lived across the street from him, and he was very much a gentleman. And if I happened to be walking up from school or if he was going by, he would always tip his hat. Men always wore hats. He would tip his hat. He would do that to me, and I always thought that was elegant.

Selected Books
in Print

1994—*Shadowmaker* (Delacorte)

1994—*My Baby* (Houston and Harris County Mental Health Association)

1994—*A Dangerous Promise* (Bantam Doubleday Dell)

1995—*The Casebusters #1: The Statue that Walks at Night* (Hyperion/Disney Press)

1995—*The Casebusters #2: The Legend of the Lost Mine* (Hyperion/ Disney)

1995—*The Casebusters #3: Backstage with a Ghost* (Hyperion/ Disney)

1995—*The Casebusters #4: Check in to Danger* (Hyperion/Disney)

1995—*Keeping Secrets* (Bantam Doubleday Dell)

1995—*Spirit Seeker* (Delacorte)

1996—*Don't Scream* (Delacorte)

1996—*The Casebusters #5: The House Has Eyes* (Disney)

1996—*The Casebusters #6: No Time for Danger* (Disney)

1996—*The Casebusters #7: Beware of the Pirate Ghost* (Disney)

1996—*The Casebusters #8: Catch a Crooked Clown* (Disney)

1996—*The Casebusters #9: Fear Stalks Grizzly Hill* (Disney)

1996—*The Casebusters #10: Sabotage on the Set* (Disney)

1996—*Search for the Shadowman* (Delacorte)

1997—*Murdered, My Sweet* (Delacorte)

1997—*The Casebusters #11: The Internet Escapade* (Disney)

1997—The Casebusters #12: Bait for a Burglar
(Disney)

1997—A Circle of Love (Bantam Doubleday Dell)

1998—The Haunting (Delacorte)

1998—Orphan Train Children: Lucy's Wish (Bantam
Doubleday Dell)

1998—Orphan Train Children: David's Search
(Bantam Doubleday Dell)

1998—Orphan Train Children: Aggie's Home (Bantam
Doubleday Dell)

1999—Orphan Train Children: Will's Choice (Bantam
Doubleday Dell)

1998—My Promise (Houston and Harris County
Mental Health Association)

1998—Champagne at the Murder. Co-author Kathleen
Nixon Brush (NTC/Contemporary Publishing
Company)

1999—Champagne at Risk. Co-author Kathleen Nixon
Brush. (NTC/Contemporary)

1999—Champagne with a Corpse. Co-author Kathleen
Nixon Brush. (NTC/Contemporary)

1999—Who Are You? (Bantam Doubleday Dell)

2000—Ghost Town (Bantam Doubleday Dell)

2000—Gus and Gertie and the Missing Pearl
(North/South Books)

2000—Young American's Series: Ann's Story: 1747
(Random House)

2000—Young American's Series: Caesar's Story: 1759
(Random House)

2000—Young American's Series: Nancy's Story: 1765
(Random House)

2001—*Young American's Series: Will's Story: 1771*
    (Random House)

2001—*Young American's Series: Maria's Story: 1773*
    (Random House)

2001—*Young American's Series: John's Story: 1775*
    (Random House)

2001—*Gus and Gertie and the Lucky Charms*
    (North/South Books)

2001—*Playing for Keeps* (Random House)

2002—*The Trap* (Random House)

2002—*The Making of a Writer* (Random House)

2003—*Nightmare*

2004—*Laugh Until You Cry*

Selected Out-of-Print Titles

1964—*The Mystery of Hurricane Castle*. Illustrated by Velam Ilsley (Criterion)

1965—*The Mystery of the Grinning Idol*. Illustrated by Alvin Smith (Criterion)

1966—*The Mystery of the Hidden Cockatoo*. Illustrated by Richard Lewis (Criterion)

1968—*The Mystery of the Secret Stowaway*. Illustrated by Joan Drescher (Criterion)

1974—*The Alligator Under the Bed*. Illustrated by Jan Hughes (Putnam)

1975—*The Mysterious Red Tape Gang*. Illustrated by Joan Sandin (Putnam)

1977—*Oil and Gas, From Fossils to Fuels*. With Hershell H. Nixon (Harcourt)

1978—*Volcanoes: Nature's Fireworks*. With Hershell H. Nixon (Dodd Mead)

1980—*Glaciers: Nature's Frozen Rivers*. With Hershell H. Nixon (Dodd Mead)

1980—*If You Say So, Claude*. Illustrated by Lorinda Bryan Cauley (Warne)

1981—*Earthquakes: Nature in Motion*. With Hershell H. Nixon (Dodd Mead)

1985—*Land Under the Sea*. With Hershell H. Nixon (Dodd Mead)

1986—*Beats Me, Claude.* Illustrated by Tracey
Campbell Pearson (Viking)

1987—*Fat Chance, Claude.* Illustrated by Tracey
Campbell Pearson (Viking)

1989—*You Bet Your Britches, Claude.* Illustrated by
Tracey Campbell Pearson (Viking)

1991—*The Mystery Box* (The Nic-Nacs) (Dell)

1991—*The Honeycutt Street Celebrities* (The Nic-Nacs)
(Dell)

1991—*The Haunted House on Honeycutt Street* (The
Nic-Nacs) (Dell)

1991—*High Trail to Danger* (Bantam)

1992—*That's the Spirit, Claude* (Viking)

1992—*Land of Hope* (Bantam)

1993—*Land of Promise* (Bantam)

1994—*Land of Dreams* (Delacorte)

Book Awards

Edgar Allan Poe Award (Mystery Writers of America)

The Kidnapping of Christina Lattimore	1980
The Séance	1981
The Other Side of Dark	1986
The Name of the Game Was Murder	1994

Spur Award (Western Writers of America)

A Family Apart	1988
In the Face of Danger	1989

Children's Choice Awards (by state)

Arizona Young Readers' Award

The Name of the Game Was Murder	1997

California Young Reader's Medal

The Stalker	1989
The Other Side of Dark	1990

Colorado's Blue Spruce Award

The Other Side of Dark	1988

Indiana's Young Hoosier Book Award

A Deadly Game of Magic	1988
The Dark and Deadly Pool	1990
The Weekend Was Murder!	1996

Iowa's Teen Award

The Other Side of Dark	1988

Maryland's Black-Eyed Susan Award

The Name of the Game Was Murder — 1997

Nebraska's Golden Sower Award

Whispers from the Dead — 1993

The Haunting — 2001

Nevada's Young Readers Award

Whispers from the Dead — 1992

The Name of the Game Was Murder — 1996

Oklahoma's Sequoyah Young Adults Award

The Other Side of Dark — 1989

Utah's Young Adult Award

The Other Side of Dark — 1991

Virginia's Young Readers Award

The Other Side of Dark — 1989

A Family Apart — 1992

Spirit Seeker — 2000

Wyoming's Soaring Eagle Young Adult Award

Whispers from the Dead — 1996

Other Awards:

Texas Institute of Letters Award

The Alligator Under the Bed — 1975

Detroit Author Day Award

Whispers from the Dead — 1994

International Reading Association's Paul A. Witty Award for short story

"Hannah's Promise,"
in *Scholastic Scope* Magazine — 1995

Lifetime Awards:

The Kerlan Award, University of Minnesota,
Author's contribution to children's literature   *2002*

The St. Katharine Drexel Award, Catholic Library Association, High School Libraries Section,
for outstanding contribution to the field of
young adult literature   *2002*

Award Nomination/Finalist/Runner-up

Edgar Allan Poe Award (Mystery Writers of America)

The Mysterious Red Tape Gang (nomination)   *1975*
The Ghosts of Now (nomination)   *1985*
The Weekend Was Murder! (nomination)   *1993*
Shadowmaker (nomination)   *1995*
Spirit Seeker (nomination)   *1996*

Spur Award (Western Writers of America)

High Trail to Danger (finalist)   *1992*
A Dangerous Promise (finalist)   *1995*
Keeping Secrets (finalist)   *1996*

Willa Award (Women Writing the West)

Aggie's Home (finalist)   *1999*
Ghost Town (finalist)   *2001*

Crown Award, Children's (National Christian School Association)

Lucy's Wish (runner-up)   *2001*

Timeline

1927—Born, Los Angeles, California, February 3.

1938—Poem printed in *Children's Activities*

1944—First paid article in *Ford Times*

1949—Marriage to Hershell (Nick) Nixon

1950—Kathleen born

1954—Maureen born

1956—Joe born

1958—Eileen born

1961—Attended writers' conference in Corpus Christi, Texas.

1964—First book, *Mystery of Hurricane Castle*, published

1975—Texas Institute of Letters, *The Alligator Under the Bed*

1980—Edgar Award, *The Kidnapping of Christina Lattimore*

1981—Edgar Award, *The Séance*

1986—Edgar Award, *The Other Side of Dark*

1988—Spur Award, *A Family Apart*

1989—Spur Award, *In the Face of Danger*

1994—Edgar Award, *The Name of the Game Was Murder*

1997–98—President, Mystery Writers of America

1998—Kids-Love-A-Mystery Week initiated

1998—Girl Scout Delta Kappa patch created

2002—Kerlan Award for contribution to children's literature

2003—Died on June 28.

Chapter Notes

Chapter 1. Ideas Out of the Ordinary

1. Joan Lowery Nixon, e-mail to author, February 27, 2003.
2. Elizabeth S. Watson, *"The Haunting,"* review, *Horn Book*, November–December, 1998, p. 737.
3. Joan Lowery Nixon, "Kerlan Award 2002," speech, University of Minnesota, Minneapolis, MN, April 6, 2002.
4. Author interview with Joan Lowery Nixon, October 26, 2002; Joan Lowery Nixon, e-mail to author, February 20, 2003.
5. Joan Lowery Nixon, "About Joan Lowery Nixon," typescript, 2002.
6. Mary Blount Christian, e-mail to author, December 22, 2002.
7. Joan Lowery Nixon, letter to author, October 7, 2002.
8. Author interview with Joan Lowery Nixon, February 3, 2003.
9. Nixon, letter to author, October 7, 2002.
10. Ibid.
11. "Career Spotlight: Joan Lowery Nixon, author," online interview with Girl Scouts of America, n.d., <http://jfg.girlscouts.org/How/Careers/jnixon/jnixonau.htm> (September 28, 2002).; Eileen Nixon McGowan, e-mail to author, December 26, 2002.

12. Teri S. Lesesne, Lois Buckman, and Rosemary Chance, "Books for Adolescents," *Journal of Adolescent & Adult Literacy*, vol. 39:8, May 1996, p. 686.
13. Nixon, letter to author, October 7, 2002.
14. Author interview with Joan Lowery Nixon, September 26, 2002.
15. Nixon, "About Joan Lowery Nixon;" Joan Lowery Nixon, e-mail to author, February 5, 2002.
16. Lesesne, p. 687.
17. Nixon, letter to author, October 7, 2002; Joan Lowery Nixon, "Writing the Western Novel for Young Adults," *The Writer*, June 1992, p. 22.
18. "Joan Lowery Nixon Interview Transcript," Authors Online Library, 1996, <http://teacher.scholastic.com/authorsandbooks/authors/nixon/tscript.htm> (January 29, 2002).
19. Ibid.
20. Linda M. Pavonetti, "Joan Lowery Nixon: The grande dame of young adult mystery," *Journal of Adolescent & Adult Literacy*, vol. 39:6, March 1996, p. 457.
21. Joan Lowery Nixon, "Writing Mysteries Young Adults Want to Read," *The Writer*, July 1991, p. 18.
22. Ibid., p. 19.
23. Ibid., p. 20.
24. "Career Spotlight: Joan Lowery Nixon, author."
25. Lesesne, p. 688.
26. Kevin S. Hile, ed. "Joan Lowery Nixon," *Authors & Artists for Young Adults* (Detroit, MI: Gale Research Inc., 1994), vol. 12, p. 161.
27. Nixon, "About Joan Lowery Nixon."
28. McGowan, e-mail, December 26, 2002.
29. Nixon, "About Joan Lowery Nixon."

30. Melissa Fletcher Stoeltje, "MURDER FOR GENTLE READERS: Author Joan Lowery Nixon is the grande dame of young adult mysteries," *Houston Chronicle*, June 20, 1993, Texas Magazine, p. 8.

31. "The Kerlan Collection," University of Minnesota Children's Literature Research Collections, 2002, <http://special.lib.umn.edu/clrc;kerlan.htn-d> (September 28, 2002).

32. Nixon, "About Joan Lowery Nixon."

33. Ibid.

34. Joan Lowery Nixon, "Kerlan Award 2002."

Chapter 2. Reading at Age Three

1. Author interview with Joan Lowery Nixon, September 26, 2002.

2. "Nixon, Joan Lowery," *Something About the Author* (Detroit, MI: Gale Research Inc., 2000), vol. 115, p. 145.

3. Joan Lowery Nixon, *The Making of a Writer* (New York: Delacorte Press, 2002), pp. 5–6.

4. Author interview with Joan Lowery Nixon, September 26, 2002; Hile, pp. 163–164.

5. Author interview with Joan Lowery Nixon, September 26, 2002.

6. Patricia Lowery Collins, e-mail to author, January 17, 2003.

7. Author interview with Joan Lowery Nixon, February 3, 2003.

8. Author interview with Joan Lowery Nixon, September 26, 2002.

9. Ibid.

10. Ibid.

11. Ibid.

12. Nixon, letter to author, October 7, 2002.

13. Author interview with Joan Lowery Nixon, September 26, 2002.

14. Ibid.
15. Collins, e-mail, January 17, 2003.
16. Ibid.; Joan Lowery Nixon, "Various questions," e-mail to author, February 1, 2003.
17. Hile, p. 164.
18. Author interview with Joan Lowery Nixon, February 3, 2003.
19. Author interview with Joan Lowery Nixon, September 26, 2002.

Chapter 3. Published Author!

1. Author interview with Joan Lowery Nixon, September 26, 2002.
2. Hile, p. 164; Nixon, *The Making of a Writer*, p. 21.
3. Collins, e-mail, January 17, 2003.
4. Author interview with Joan Lowery Nixon, September 26, 2002.
5. Ibid.
6. "Pat Lowery Collins, My Life," n.d., <http://www.patlowerycollins.com/bio.htm> (January 21, 2003); Nixon, *The Making of a Writer*, p. 43.
7. "Nixon, Joan Lowery," *Something About the Author*, p. 148–149; Author interview with Joan Lowery Nixon, September 26, 2002.
8. Nixon, *The Making of a Writer*, p. 57; Joan Lowery Nixon, e-mail to author, December 18, 2002.
9. Author interview with Joan Lowery Nixon, September 26, 2002.
10. Ibid.
11. Hile, p. 165.
12. Author interview with Joan Lowery Nixon, September 26, 2002.
13. Nixon, e-mail to author, December 18, 2002.
14. Nixon, e-mail to author, February 1, 2003.

15. Barbara Karkabi, "Interviewing Authors," *Houston Chronicle*, October 14, 1999, p. 4.
16. Hile, p. 165.
17. Nixon, e-mail to author, December 18, 2002.
18. Nixon, *The Making of a Writer*, p. 72.
19. Author interview with Joan Lowery Nixon, September 26, 2002.
20. Ibid.
21. Nixon, e-mail to author, December 18, 2002.
22. Author interview with Joan Lowery Nixon, September 26, 2002.
23. Ibid.
24. Hile, p. 165.
25. Author interview with Joan Lowery Nixon, September 26, 2002.
26. Joan Lowery Nixon, speech, Society of Children's Book Writers and Illustrators, Houston, TX, May 6, 2002.

Chapter 4. Family Matters

1. Author interview with Joan Lowery Nixon, September 26, 2002.
2. Ibid.
3. Ibid.; Author interview with Joan Lowery Nixon, February 3, 2003.
4. Author interview with Joan Lowery Nixon, September 26, 2002.
5. Hile, p. 165.
6. Nixon, e-mail to author, February 1, 2003.
7. Ibid.
8. Author interview with Hershell Nixon, October 26, 2002.
9. Author interview with Joan Lowery Nixon, September 26, 2002.
10. Ibid.
11. Ibid.

12. Ibid.

13. Ibid.

14. Ibid.

15. Ibid.

Chapter 5. Make Them Shiver

1. Collins, e-mail to author, January 17, 2003; Nixon, *The Making of a Writer*, p. 11; *Scholastic Authors Online*, "Joan Lowery Nixon Interview Transcript," n.d., <http://teacher.scholastic.com/authorsandbooks/authors/nixon/tscript.htm> (January 29, 2002); Joan Lowery Nixon, e-mail to author, October 15, 2002.

2. Stoeltje, "MURDER FOR GENTLE READERS"; "Mystery Writers of America: A Historical Survey," 2000, <http://www.mysterywriters.org/library/mwa_history.html> (January 26, 2003); "Search the Edgar Award Winner and Nominees," n.d., <http://64.57.86.186/edgarsDB/edgarDB.php> (January 26, 2003).

3. Nixon, e-mail to author, February 1, 2003; Telephone interview with Judy Crawford, January 25, 2003.

4. Author interview with Joan Lowery Nixon, September 26, 2002.

5. Nixon, letter to author, October 7, 2002.

6. "Nixon, Joan Lowery," *Something About the Author*, p. 150.

7. Author interview with Joan Lowery Nixon, September 26, 2002; "Search the Edgar Award Winner and Nominees."

8. Maureen Nixon Quinlan, e-mail to author, December 18, 2002; "Nixon, Joan Lowery," *Something About the Author*, p. 150.

9. Nixon, speech, Society of Children's Book Writers and Illustrators, May 6, 2002.

10. Hile, p. 166.
11. Nixon, "About Joan Lowery Nixon"; "Nixon, Joan Lowery," *Something About the Author*, p. 150.
12. Lesesne, pp. 687–688.
13. Ibid., p. 687; Author interview with Joan Lowery Nixon, September 26, 2002.
14. Joan Lowery Nixon, "Talking with you about bio," e-mail to author, February 1, 2002.
15. Nixon, speech, Society of Children's Book Writers and Illustrators, May 6, 2002.
16. Nixon, "About Joan Lowery Nixon."
17. Ann Hodges, "Author braces for TV premiere," *Houston Chronicle*, March 11, 1995, Houston section, p. 1; Author interview with Joan Lowery Nixon, September 26, 2002.
18. Nixon, "About Joan Lowery Nixon"; Priscilla Ridgway, e-mail to author, February 27, 2003.
19. Hodges, p. 1.
20. Nixon, letter to author, October 7, 2002; "Meet Authors and Illustrators: Joan Lowery Nixon," n.d., <http://www.childrenslit.com/ f_joanlowerynixon.html> (September 28, 2002).
21. Quinlan, e-mail to author, December 18, 2002.
22. Author interview with Joan Lowery Nixon, October 26, 2002.
23. Author interview with Joan Lowery Nixon, September 26, 2002.
24. Ibid.
25. Ibid.
26. *Scholastic Authors Online*, "Joan Lowery Nixon Interview Transcript," n.d., <http://teacher. scholastic.com/authorsandbooks/authors/nixon/ tscript.htm> (January 29, 2002); Author interview with Joan Lowery Nixon, October 26, 2002.
27. Stoeltje, "MURDER FOR GENTLE READERS."

28. Vivienne Heines, "Mystery, they wrote," *Houston Chronicle*, November 9, 1986, Lifestyle, p. 1.

29. Ken Tucker, "Nameless Fear Stalks the Middle-Class Teen-Ager: Perhaps It Is the Fear of Boredom," *The New York Times Book Review*, November 14, 1993, pp. 29–30.

Chapter 6. The Heart of History

1. Nixon, "Writing Mysteries Young Adults Want to Read," *The Writer*, p. 23.

2. Bob Tutt, "Orphan trains took children of another era to new lives," *Houston Chronicle*, May 29, 1988, sec. 3, p. 1.

3. Nixon, "Writing the Western Novel for Young Adults," *The Writer*, p. 22.

4. Ibid.; The Children's Aid Society, "The Orphan Train Movement," 2001, <http://www.childrensaidsociety.org/about/train/> (December 24, 2002).

5. Ibid.

6. Ibid.

7. Nixon, "Kerlan Award, 2002"; Tutt.

8. The Children's Aid Society, "The Orphan Train Movement."

9. Author interview with Joan Lowery Nixon, September 26, 2002.

10. Joan Lowery Nixon, writers' panel, Women Writing the West, Denver CO., October 26, 2002.

11. Author interview with Joan Lowery Nixon, September 26, 2002.

12. Ibid.

13. Mary Ellen Johnson, "History of the ORPHAN TRAIN HERITAGE SOCIETY OF AMERICA, Inc.," 1997, <http://www.orphantrainriders.com/othsa11.html> (January 31, 2003).

14. Nixon, writers' panel, Women Writing the West, Denver, Colorado, October 26, 2002.
15. "Joan Lowery Nixon," teachers@random, 2002, <http://www.randomhouse.com/teachers/authors/nixo.html> (January 29, 2002).
16. Joan Lowery Nixon, *A Family Apart* (New York: Bantam Books, 1987), p. 47.
17. Nixon, writers' panel, Women Writing the West, Denver, Colorado, October 26, 2002.
18. Nixon, "About Joan Lowery Nixon."
19. Ibid.
20. Author interview with Joan Lowery Nixon, September 26, 2002.
21. Ibid.
22. Ibid.
23. Ibid.
24. Ibid.
25. Ibid.
26. Ibid.
27. Ibid.
28. Ibid.

Chapter 7. Fun and Facts

1. Joan Lowery Nixon, *Fat Chance, Claude* (New York: Viking, 1987) n.p.
2. Author interview with Hershell Nixon, October 26, 2002.
3. "Nixon, Joan Lowery," *Something About the Author*, p. 115.
4. Stoeltje, "MURDER FOR GENTLE READERS."

Chapter 8. Consider the Children

1. Author interview with Joan Lowery Nixon, September 26, 2002.
2. Ibid.
3. Ibid.

4. Joan Lowery Nixon, together with the Houston Alumnae Association of Kappa Delta Sorority, *My Baby* (Houston: The Mental Health Association of Greater Houston, 1993), unp.

5. Ibid.

6. Leslie Sowers, "My Promise: Writer vows to reach young mothers and help foster confidence," *Houston Chronicle*, December 6, 1998, Lifestyle, p. 4.

7. Joan Lowery Nixon, together with the Houston Alumnae Association of Kappa Delta Sorority, *My Promise*, (Houston: The Mental Health Association of Greater Houston, 1998), unp.

8. Terri Urbina, letter to author, December 23, 2002.

9. Ibid., Author interview with Joan Lowery Nixon, September 26, 2002.

10. Sowers, "My Promise. . ."; Urbina, letter to author, December 23, 2002.

11. Joan Lowery Nixon, e-mail to author, September 29, 2002; "Houston's Nixon to lead writers group," *Houston Chronicle*, March 2, 1997, Zest, p. 28.

12. "Kids Love A Mystery.com," 2003, <http://www.kidsloveamystery.com> (September 28, 2002); Joan Lowery Nixon, e-mail to author, January 22, 2003.

13. "Career Spotlight: Joan Lowery Nixon, author."

14. Ellen Godfrey, "Mystery and Literacy," 1998, <http://www.ellengodfrey.com/Literacy.html> (September 28, 2002).

15. Kathleen Nixon Brush, letter to author, January 4, 2003.

16. Quinlan, e-mail to author, December 18, 2002.

17. Patti Keplinger, e-mail to author, January 7, 2003.

18. Melinda Gaskill, e-mail to author, January 23, 2003.
19. Keplinger, e-mail to author, January 7, 2003.

Chapter 9. The Gift of Reading

1. McGowan, e-mail to author, December 26, 2002.
2. Barbara Karkabi, "Timely books offer differing views of motherhood," *Houston Chronicle*, May 10, 1998, Lifestyle, p. 5.
3. Carol Gorman, e-mail to author, December 8, 2002.
4. Stoeltje, "MURDER FOR GENTLE READERS."
5. Author interview with Joan Lowery Nixon, February 3, 2003; Joan Lowery Nixon, e-mail to author, February 15, 2003.
6. Nixon, *The Making of a Writer*, pp. 1–2.
7. Mary Blount Christian, e-mail to author, December 22, 2002.
8. Author interview with Joan Lowery Nixon, September 26, 2002.
9. Brush, letter to author, January 4, 2003.
10. Charles Trevino, e-mail to author, February 27, 2003; Society of Children's Book Writers and Illustrators - Houston, *Picturing the Write Stuff*, January/February 2003, p. 4.
11. "Joan Lowery Nixon Interview Transcript."
12. Nixon, "Writing Mysteries Young Adults Want to Read," p. 20.
13. Thomas, Sherry, "There's a Story Behind Writer's Last Mystery," *Houston Chronicle*, October 9, 2003; Phone interview with Beverly Horowitz, editor, Knopf Delacorte Dell Young Readers Group, October 15, 2003.

Words to Know

accelerated—Speeded up.

artifacts—An object made by a person in a different time or culture.

aspiring—Wishing to be.

auditor-comptroller—An official in government or business who oversees how money is spent.

ceramic—Made of clay heated to a high temperature, like pottery or china.

coma—A long state of unconsciousness due to illness or injury.

chaperone—A person who accompanies a person or group and is responsible for their welfare.

child services—A government agency that protects young children from abuse.

cockatoo—A bird with a large crest of feathers.

compulsory—Something that is required.

culprit—A guilty person.

dedicated word processor—A computer that will only type words.

duplex—Two houses joined by a common wall or passage.

fashion column—Recurring newspaper articles that report on the latest clothes.

foundling—An orphan or abandoned child.

foyer—Entrance of a building.

garment district—The area of New York City with factories that made clothing; often the only place where immigrants were able to get work.

graphics—Illustrations and decorative parts of a book.

hitch—A period of military service.

in the thick—In the middle, usually referring to a boisterous or confused situation.

initiate—To begin an action.

irrepressible—Hard to control.

journalism—Collecting information and writing news articles.

jump seat—A seat in a car that folds up when not in use.

Montessori—A method of teaching young children that encourages creativity and initiative; based on the ideas of Maria Montessori.

moral—Having good character and acceptable behavior.

myrtles—Flowering shrubs that grow in the southern part of the United States.

niche—A place or situation especially suited for a person.

overwhelmed—Overpowered; unable to act because of circumstances.

paddlewheeler—Old-fashioned riverboat driven by a huge revolving wheel at the rear.

pancreatic cancer—Cancer of the pancreas, the body
    organ that produces a fluid to aid in digestion.

paper drives—A conservation effort to collect paper for
    re-use.

pinafore—A sleeveless jumper dress that has a bib in the
    front like an apron.

plucky—Showing courage or resourcefulness when in a
    bad situation; spunky.

savvy—Smart.

sorority—A social or civic club for women.

spunky—Spirited; plucky.

stowaway—A person who hides aboard a ship in order
    to avoid paying the fare.

subconscious—The state of not being fully conscious, as
    in thoughts that are in your mind but you may not
    be aware of them.

synchronized swimming—A water ballet where swimmers'
    movements are together.

taut—Pulled very tight.

tempo—Speed.

tenement—Rundown apartment houses where workers
    lived.

unconditional—Having no restrictions.

upscale—Fancy; expensive.

waif—Abandoned young child.

war correspondent—A reporter who sends news from war
    zones.

Further Reading

Nixon, Joan Lowery. *The Making of a Writer*. New York: Delacorte Press, 2002.

"Nixon, Joan Lowery," *Something About the Author*. vol. 115. Detroit: Gale Research Inc., 2000, pp. 145–154 .

Internet Addresses

"Joan Lowery Nixon," teachers@random, 2002
http://www.randomhouse.com/teachers/authors/results.pperl?authorid=22240

"Joan Lowery Nixon," Authors Online Library, 2002
http://www2.scholastic.com/teachers/authorsandbooks/authorstudies/authorstudies.jhtml?IndexLetter=N

Kids Love A Mystery.com
http://www.kidsloveamystery.com

Index